KINGDOM HEROES
FOR KIDS

TONY EVANS

ILLUSTRATED BY COLE ROBERTS

HARVEST HOUSE PUBLISHERS
EUGENE, OREGON

Cover and interior illustrations by Cole Roberts
Cover design by Bryce Williamson
Interior design by KUHN Design Group

For bulk, special sales, or ministry purchases, please call 1-800-547-8979.
Email: Customerservice@hhpbooks.com

ᴍ is a federally registered trademark of the Hawkins Children's LLC. Harvest House Publishers, Inc., is the exclusive licensee of the trademark.

Kingdom Heroes for Kids
Copyright © 2022 by Tony Evans
Published by Harvest House Publishers
Eugene, Oregon 97408
www.harvesthousepublishers.com

ISBN 978-0-7369-8514-7 (pbk.)
ISBN 978-0-7369-8515-4 (eBook)

Library of Congress Control Number: 2022931408

Printed in the United States of America

22 23 24 25 26 27 28 29 30 / VP / 10 9 8 7 6 5 4 3 2 1

CONTENTS

KINGDOM HEROES

Who They Are, What They Do

Have you ever heard the expression "throwing in the towel"? People say this when they're just *done* trying to make something work. You can "throw in the towel" on trying to understand your math homework. You can "throw in the towel" on attempting to figure out that really hard song on the piano. You can "throw in the towel" on having the same conversation over and over with the friend you're always arguing with.

Over it.

Finished.

Not gonna work.

Ever.

Guess what? Sometimes it's okay to give up. Put that math homework aside until you can ask your teacher or your tutor for help—especially if your mom (who's trying to help you) says for the forty-seventh time, "Hang on, I *think* I remember how to do this!" Go back to an easier piano piece and play it over and over again until your confidence is back up. Take a break from constantly texting your on-again, off-again friend so both of you can take some time to figure out how to make your friendship better.

But you should *never* throw in the towel on one thing:

God.

That's because God is always, always there for you. He's more amazing than you can imagine, but He's not confusing, like your math homework. He's not going to keep frustrating you, like your challenging piano piece. And His friendship with you is always *on*, unlike your flaky friend.

What things in your life have you wanted to quit, but you kept going? Write them down here. Who or what convinced you to keep going? Are you happy you didn't quit? _____

_____

_____

_____

_____

_____

_____

_____

_____

_____

_____

_____

HOW TO BE A HERO

If you want to be someone who keeps going when life gets hard—someone who pushes through instead of giving up or throwing in the towel—keep reading!

In the pages of the Bible, you can meet people who kept going and pushed through the hard times. I like to call these people "kingdom heroes" because that's exactly who they were—heroes for the kingdom of God. They were also people just like you and me. They sometimes got frustrated. They often felt like quitting. They didn't always get along with everyone around them.

But they were heroes because they kept their faith in God. They never gave up on Him. Sure, they probably had some intense conversations with Him and asked Him a lot of questions, like "God, what in the world are You *doing*? None of this makes any sense!" Yet they trusted in Him and chose to do things His way.

Those two things are all it takes to be a kingdom hero: Trusting in God and choosing to do things His way.

> *What it takes to be a kingdom hero:*
> *1. Trust in God.*
> *2. Choose to do things His way.*

Hebrews 10:35-39 gives us some helpful hints on what it takes to live as a kingdom hero:

So do not throw away your confidence; it will be richly rewarded.

You need to persevere so that when you have done the will of God, you will receive what he has promised. For,

> "In just a little while,
>   he who is coming will come
>   and will not delay."

And,

> "But my righteous one will live by faith.
>   And I take no pleasure
>   in the one who shrinks back."

But we do not belong to those who shrink back and are destroyed, but to those who have faith and are saved.

Write down Hebrews 10:35-39 in your own words. You can even draw pictures or write it the same way you would send a text. What is God trying to tell *you* through these verses? _____

_____

_____

_____

_____

_____

_____

_____

_____

_____

_____

These verses might be a little hard to understand, but they show us one of the things we need the most to help us live our lives as kingdom heroes—*endurance*. People who have endurance keep going. You need endurance for a lot of things in life. Playing a sport requires endurance. So does being in a play. Or writing a long paper for school. Or knitting a scarf. Or making cinnamon rolls. Being a good friend also requires endurance. And so does following Jesus.

Jesus promises us that if we have faith in Him, He will give us endurance. If you want to be a kingdom hero, you need to ask yourself a very important question:

Am I living by faith?

You need to start here. You need to start with *you* because if living by faith isn't how you roll, learning about the kingdom heroes in the Bible isn't going to help you.

Right now, let's take a little break from reading and pray this prayer together:

> *Dear Jesus, please help me to have faith in You—*
> *and help me to get to know You better so I can see all*
> *the amazing ways I can live my life for You! Thank*
> *You for making me one of Your kingdom heroes!*

SO WHAT EXACTLY IS A KINGDOM HERO?

Here's a great definition of a kingdom hero. (Hint: It's something you might want to write down so you can come back to it.)

A kingdom hero is a committed Christian (someone who follows Christ all the way) who lives by faith in order to experience spiritual victory and God's approval.

(By the way, both girls and boys can be heroes! Sometimes girls are called "heroines," but we'll just make it simple and use the word "hero" for everyone. In the coming pages, you'll meet both women and men of faith who are kingdom heroes.)

Let's talk a little more about faith, because faith is the key to living the hero life. Faith isn't just a feeling or an idea or something that's impossible to understand.

If you have kingdom faith, it means you are absolutely, completely, 100 percent sure of the things you hope for. You don't know exactly what will happen, but you have *faith* that good things are going to happen. And you know that these things are *good* because they are from *God*. You have *faith* that His plan is the best plan, and so you choose to do what He asks you to do.

Can you think of a movie or a book where a character faced a lot of challenges and pushed through to the happy ending? That's a good example of living life as a kingdom hero! The character found herself in some impossible situations, but she refused to throw in the towel, and it all worked out in the end.

FAITH AND THE FIVE SENSES

Can you name the five senses? Write them down here.

_____

_____

_____

_____

_____

What are some things you can do with each of your five senses? List those things here. _____

_____

_____

_____

_____

_____

_____

_____

_____

_____

_____

You can't really use any of your five senses for faith. That's because while the five senses have to do with the *physical* realm—the things you can see or hear or touch or taste or feel here on earth—faith involves the *spiritual* realm.

Let's look at how we use our five senses during the fun tradition of receiving presents on Christmas morning or Christmas Eve. (And we'll see how this relates to faith!) A lot of things involving the Christmas celebration involve your senses. You can *see* the brightly wrapped presents under the tree. You can *touch* them (and shake them a little to try to guess what's inside!). You can *smell* the fresh scent of evergreen if your family puts up a real tree. (You can also smell winter-scented candles or seasonal treats baking in the oven.) You can *hear* your favorite Christmas carols and songs. You can *taste* the cookies or cinnamon rolls and hot cocoa your family enjoys while opening gifts. But none of these things really guarantee that when you unwrap the present, there will be something in it for you. Opening presents involves *faith* that the person who gave you the gift has put something inside you will like!

You can't see or touch or smell or hear or taste the act of giving. You can use your five senses to *assume* that you'll receive a gift, but you need to have *faith* that something is in the package for you.

When you open a Christmas present, you both *expect* and *hope* that the present is something you will like—and your expectation and hope are based on *faith*. You believe that something will happen even though you can't *see* it happening ahead of time.

PUT YOUR FAITH IN WHAT IS REAL

It's important to have faith, but we need to be careful not to put our faith in things that aren't really *real*. Like believing that wearing what's trendy will make you happy. Or that being in a popular friend group will change your life. Or even that taking a trip to Disneyland will make you the happiest person on earth. These things might make you happy in the moment, but they aren't guaranteed to make your life better forever.

A lot of faith placed in something that doesn't really matter will end up doing nothing. That's because what makes faith work is the thing to which it's attached. So if you want to grow your faith, you need to put your faith in something real and unchanging. And that something is God.

You can't literally see or hear or touch or taste or smell God. But He is always there. And you can always put your faith in Him.

BIG PLANE = BIG FAITH

My wife, Lois, often traveled with me on my speaking trips, but she didn't want to go on this one trip to Iowa because we'd be flying in a small, twin-engine plane.

"You don't have much faith," I said, joking with her.

"That's because you don't have much plane," she responded.

Not until the schedule changed and Lois found out that our

new flight would be on a jumbo jet did she change her mind and come along.

"Your faith grew," I told her, laughing as we boarded the much larger plane.

"That's because your plane grew," she said, smiling in response.

It's a humorous story, but you get the point. The size of my wife's faith was directly tied to the size of the plane. Big plane = big faith. That's because faith is related to whatever it's attached to. Big God = big faith!

FAITH IN ACTION

Before we start getting to know the kingdom heroes in the Bible, I want to give you a simple definition of faith:

Faith is basing your actions on the belief that what God says is true.

Write down what you think it means to have faith. Then make a list of ways you can put that faith into action. What specific things can you do to show that you have faith in God? Be creative with your answers!_____

_____

Faith isn't just *feeling* like God is telling the truth. Faith isn't just *saying* that God is telling the truth. For faith to truly be faith, it's *acting* like God is telling the truth. That's why the Bible calls it *walking* by faith, not *talking* by faith or *feeling* by faith.

A few years ago, my church decided to install motion-detector lighting in certain rooms. That meant the lights would only come on when motion was detected. If there was no motion, there was no light. This also meant that the lights went off on their own when people left without turning them off. Then the lights came back on again when motion was detected.

Similarly, God will give you the power and light you need when you need it, but He'll wait until He detects motion—or *action*—on your part. If you don't move, He won't give you His power and light. But when you *do* move—or act—He gives you His power and light.

WHY DO WE NEED KINGDOM HEROES?

Why do we need heroes, anyway? Well, think about people you admire. Maybe they're famous people—like actors or musicians or athletes or artists or writers. Maybe they're people in your own life who you admire and look up to—your big brother, your grandparents, your teacher or coach, or your summer camp counselor. You see them doing amazing things, and you want to be just like them. Their lives motivate you to hang in there, never give up, and stand strong for what you believe in.

Everyone needs heroes—especially kingdom heroes!

Who do you admire and why? Write down their names and all the reasons you admire them. _____

_____

_____

_____

_____

_____

_____

_____

_____

_____

_____

_____

_____

WARNING!

Before we meet our first kingdom hero in this book, I want to warn you about something. Some of these heroes are pretty strange people. And some of them did some things that seem downright messed-up!

But that's good news for you and me. It means we don't have to be perfect in order to be a hero. No matter how many times you've messed up or made a mistake, you can start over and keep making the choice to live differently. And you can choose to do it right now! All you need to do is ask God for His help.

If you want to live as a kingdom hero, you need to do two things: Have faith in God. And then act on that faith. Remember Hebrews 11:1:

> *Now faith is confidence in what*
> *we hope for and assurance*
> *about what we do not see.*

Faith is all about what we do not see. It's all about believing that what God says is true, and then trusting God enough to do what He asks us to do.

Think about a weather forecast. If the weather experts predict a rainstorm, your actions show that you believe it's going to rain. You might wear a raincoat. Your family might reschedule an outdoor party. You might skip watering the garden because you know the rain is coming. And you know what? The weather experts are sometimes wrong, but we listen to them anyway. How much more should we listen to and trust God, who is always right?

Believe what God says is true.

Act on what you believe.

That's what kingdom heroes do!

1

ABEL

Giving God Your Best

Have you ever been to a family camp? My family used to love to go to a family camp in New York during the winter where I was the guest speaker. The camp sits on a large lake with the grown-up facilities on one side of the water and the kids' buildings on the other side.

On one of our visits to the camp, the lake was frozen, and nearly all camp activities were happening inside, where it was warm. But when it came time for me to speak to the youth, instead of suggesting we circle the lake to get to our destination, the person hosting me said we could just walk across it.

"It's shorter this way," he said.

I said nothing and just looked out at the lake, a bunch of potentially scary events playing out in my mind. I wasn't thrilled about trying to walk across any lake, even a frozen one. The thought of ice cracking beneath my feet was enough for me to stay firmly planted right where I was—on solid pavement.

My host, noticing my hesitation, pointed to a truck starting to cross the lake. And as I saw the truck being driven across the lake, my faith suddenly grew stronger. I realized that if a heavy truck could safely cross the frozen lake, surely I could walk across it.

So after a long pause and a deep breath, I set out, making the expression *walk by faith* way more personal to me than it had ever been before!

Seeing something bigger and heavier than me do something I'd been afraid to do increased my belief that I could do the same thing. That's kind of what happens when you learn about the kingdom heroes in the Bible. You read about them following God in faith and doing amazing things, and that increases your belief that you can do the same thing (especially when you realize that they weren't perfect!).

WORSHIP

When you hear the term *hero*, what words come to mind? Write them down here. (You can draw a picture of a hero too.)_____

_____

_____

_____

_____

_____

_____

_____

_____

_____

_____

_____

_____

You might have written down words like *strong* or *power* or *talent* or *brave*. But I'm guessing you probably didn't write down this word:

Worship.

Worship? What does *that* have to do with being a hero?

I'm not talking about the kind of worship most of us think of, though. I'm not talking about listening to your favorite Christian musician, or admiring God's creation when you see a pretty sunset or some cool clouds, or writing down everything you're thankful for in your prayer journal. The kind of worship I'm talking about is *honoring God through the choices you make in your life*.

> ## Worship (n.): honoring God through the choices you make in your life

This is God's definition of worship, which we can find in Romans 12:1: "Therefore, I urge you, brothers and sisters, in view of God's mercy, to offer your bodies as a living sacrifice, holy and pleasing to God—this is your true and proper worship."

According to the Bible, you worship God when you use the time, talents, and treasures He's given you for His glory. This could be something big and public like a basketball player who wins a national championship giving God the glory during a postgame interview. Or something small and private like spending an extra 15 minutes of your day playing with your little brother. God doesn't say one thing is better than the other—*both* actions show that a person is following Him.

KNOW THE STANDARD

To live by a kingdom standard—which is like a rule or a guideline—you need to know what that standard is. You can find the kingdom standards in God's Word, the Bible. God says that staying close to Him helps us live by kingdom standards. In Deuteronomy 6:4-9, He gives us directions for learning His standards and passing them on to others.

> Hear, O Israel: The LORD our God, the LORD is one. Love the LORD your God with all your heart and with all your soul and with all your strength. These commandments that I give you today are to be on your hearts. Impress them on your children. Talk about them when you sit at home and when you walk along the road, when you lie down and when you get up. Tie them as symbols on your hands and bind them on your foreheads. Write them on the doorframes of your houses and on your gates.

God gave us clear instructions on how to stay close to Him and live the way He wants us to live. God's Word should be a routine part of your everyday life, whether you are walking, sitting, coming in, or going out. In every part of your life, you should consider God and His incredible love for you. And in every part of your life, you should do your best to stay close to Him.

A SHEPHERD WHO WORSHIPPED RIGHT

You've heard the story of Cain and Abel, right? Most of us know it this way: Cain killed his brother, Abel.

Boom.

End of story.

But there's a lot more to it than that.

Abel is the first kingdom hero we're going to meet. Don't worry, though. You don't have to be killed by your brother in order to achieve hero status.

The reason Abel was killed might surprise you. He wasn't killed over an argument. He wasn't even killed over something he did to offend Cain. Nope. Abel was killed because of the way he *worshipped.*

Before this all gets way too confusing, let's look at Hebrews 11:4 to see how it all went down:

> By faith Abel brought a better offering than Cain did. By faith he was commended as righteous, when God spoke well of his offerings. And by faith Abel still speaks, even though he is dead.

Did you know that Abel was the first person ever who had the chance to live by faith? His parents, Adam and Eve, got to live in a perfect environment.

And in a perfect environment, you don't need faith! It's like if you already have a bowl of ice cream sitting in front of you, you don't need to have faith that there's some ice cream left in the freezer.

You probably remember that Abel had a brother, Cain. The two brothers had different jobs. As it says in Genesis 4:2, "Abel kept flocks, and Cain worked the soil." Abel raised animals and Cain grew stuff.

Cain and Abel were raised by parents who believed in God. Their parents had even experienced walking with God face to face "in the cool of the day" (Genesis 3:8). Because their parents loved God, Cain and Abel learned it was important to worship and honor Him.

LEARNING VERSUS DOING

I'm sure you know that learning something and doing it are two very different things. You can watch an Olympic gymnast do a floor exercise routine or see a construction crew put up a really cool building, but does that mean you can do the same gymnastics routine or create a building on your own? Of course not!

You can also be told it's really important to do something—like study for your science test or brush your teeth after every meal. But sometimes you just don't want to do it. You're too sleepy. Or you're having too much fun doing something else. But there are consequences for not doing what you were told to do. Like getting a bad grade on the test. Or having the dentist tell you that you have a mouthful of cavities. Genesis 4:3-5 shows us what happens when you make the wrong choice:

> In the course of time Cain brought some of the fruits of the soil as
> an offering to the Lord. And Abel also brought an offering—fat

portions from some of the firstborn of his flock. The LORD looked with favor on Abel and his offering, but on Cain and his offering he did not look with favor. So Cain was very angry, and his face was downcast.

Abel made the right choice. Cain made the wrong choice. Yes, both brothers brought an offering. But one did it the way God wanted it done, and the other did not.

What are some things you know you *should* do but you don't want to do? To help yourself get motivated to do these things, make a list of the good things that will happen when you make the *right* choice and do the things you don't want to do. _____

_____

_____

_____

_____

_____

_____

_____

_____

_____

_____

_____

_____

_____

Cain and Abel both knew what God wanted and how He wanted it done. But Cain chose to test the limits. He wanted to do things his own way. God said that the offering needed to be a slain animal. But Cain wanted to take the easy route. So he quickly gathered up some tomatoes, cabbage, and whatever fruit he had and brought it to God. Then he tossed it on the altar and said, "Here You go, God!"

Abel, on the other hand, did what God wanted. He brought "fat portions from some of the firstborn of his flock"—the very best he had available. He brought a *sacrifice*. He gave God what He had asked for. And that's true worship.

God accepted Abel's offering. But not Cain's. God said, "I'm not doing anything with that, Cain. It's unacceptable."

KINGDOM HERO SPOTLIGHT

Samson (Judges 13:24–16:31)

Samson was a complicated man who made some really bad choices. He constantly messed up. Yet even though he failed in many areas, whenever he was willing to operate by faith, he was able to do great things to accomplish God's will.

The Bible tells us that Samson killed a thousand men with the jawbone of a donkey. He was a beast on the battlefield. What's more, he killed more of his enemies on the day of his death than he'd defeated in all his years. Samson went out in a blaze even though he'd struggled with a lot of issues throughout his life. Yes, there were consequences to Samson's bad actions. But when he was willing to be useful to God, his actions allowed God to show up when the Israelites needed Him the most.

WORSHIP IS ABOUT JESUS

I'm happy to report that today, we don't need to bring God animal sacrifices to show Him that we worship and honor Him.

Today, our worship is about Jesus, who died on the cross to pay the penalty for all of our sins. When you worship Jesus, you admit that you have sinned and that sin has affected your life. Then you ask God to forgive you for the sinful things you've done. You don't have to remember every single sin. That would be impossible! But you can probably remember a few things—like cheating on your math test or yelling at your dad—and ask God to forgive you for those things and anything else you've done wrong. Then you can worship with a clean heart.

What have you done in the past day or week that you need to ask forgiveness for? Write it down here. Then write down a prayer about it and (this part is the best!) cross it off because God has forgiven you!

_____

_____

_____

_____

_____

_____

_____

_____

_____

GIVE GOD YOUR BEST

Not only did Cain and Abel bring God different offerings—one according to the way God wanted it done and the other by taking a shortcut—but their offerings differed in another way. Abel brought the *best* of his flock. He didn't give God junk and leftovers. Cain, though, just brought "an offering." He rounded up some random fruits and veggies and called it a day.

God wants you to give Him your best. You can start doing this by making time for Him. Don't just give Him your leftovers. Talk to Him throughout the day. Don't just say a quick prayer at bedtime. Do something to remind yourself that God comes first in your life. Write a favorite verse on your school notebook. Put a sticky note on your dresser. Keep your Bible in a place where you'll notice it.

Have you ever been hanging out with a friend who just spends the whole time looking at his phone? While you're talking, he's scrolling. Or playing a game. Or texting. Then when you ask him a question, he looks up at you with a confused expression and says, "What?"

That's how a lot of us act when God is trying to tell us something important. We barely pay attention to Him, but we expect Him to always give us what we want—exactly when we want it.

Let's say you went to a restaurant with your family and the server brought out the menus and said, "Hey, we're serving whatever we couldn't sell last week! You can order any of these leftovers. We could even mix them all together in a soup!"

What would you do? Would you order something from that restaurant? Or would you walk out and find a better place to eat?

I know what I would do! I'd walk out and find a restaurant that served something better. You don't go out to eat looking for last week's leftovers. You expect better than that!

We should give God the very best we have. No leftovers when we're worshipping Him!

DON'T GIVE GOD JUNK FOOD

You know what's worse than leftovers? Junk food.

While you might like the taste of junk food, it's not good for your body. It can make you feel tired and grumpy. And too much junk food can eventually cause a whole bunch of health problems.

> Make a list of foods you *love*. Then think of how you feel when you eat those foods. Do they give you more energy, or do you feel yucky after you eat them? Cross everything off the list that could

be considered "junk food." Then add some healthier foods if your list is too small! (And remember, a lot of "healthy" foods are super yummy—like strawberries and blueberries and smoothies!)

_____

_____

_____

_____

_____

_____

_____

_____

_____

_____

_____

_____

_____

_____

_____

_____

Some people are satisfied with giving God junk food. They give Him barely anything at all—just a super-quick prayer every now and then. And mostly only when they want something. They have time for everything but God. If you have enough time to binge watch your favorite shows or spend hours on your phone or play video games, you have time for God! And you know what's really awesome? The more time you spend with God, the more time you will *want* to spend with Him as you get to know Him better and better!

Have you ever taken a back-lot tour at Universal Studios and seen the facade of buildings where films are made? They're just makeshift little towns showing only fronts. If you were to peek behind them, you'd see nothing there.

Some people might say they follow Christ, but when you look at their lives, there's nothing there. They don't pray much. They don't read their Bible. They don't tell others about Jesus. They don't *do* anything.

Heroes aren't heroes because they say they're heroes. Heroes are heroes because of what they *do*.

Worship God the way heroes worship—with all of your heart, all of your soul, and all of your mind. And worship Him in faith. This means taking God seriously. And believing that what He says in His Word is 100 percent true.

Here's one more definition of faith:

*Faith is simply acting
like God is telling the truth.*

The choices and decisions you make should reflect a heart that believes what God says is true. If we believe what God says is true, our actions will show it. But some of us live like Cain. We test the limits. We want to do things our way, not God's way. We want to take the easy path, but not following God actually puts us on the more difficult path.

ALWAYS FOR THE BEST

Does it ever seem like you're the only one in your friend group who's trying to do the right thing? As you follow God and get excited about what He's teaching you, you try to share all those great things with others. But nobody seems to be listening. Your friends continue to make fun of other kids. Or complain a ton. Or even lie to someone or cheat on a test. The more you care about doing the right thing, the less they seem to care.

Don't give up! God is always teaching you, and God is always guiding you. You don't know exactly how things will turn out, but He promises that everything will be okay. Maybe He will send some new friends your way—friends who follow God and want to do the right thing. Maybe your current friends will see that their way isn't working, and they will turn to God. Maybe a little of both will happen.

What God ends up doing is usually not quite what we think He will do. But it's always for the best.

Which of your friends aren't making good choices? Pray for these friends every day, and think of things you can do together to show them that it's fun to do the right thing!

WHAT HAPPENS WHEN YOU DON'T OBEY

I'm sure you've personally experienced what happens when you don't obey. Your mom tells you and your sister to stop fighting, but you keep right on going at each other. Until suddenly both of you have "earned" extra chores. Or your teacher warns you and your best friend to stop talking in class. But you two have so much important stuff to say to each other! Before you know it, your BFF has been moved to the other side of the classroom.

When you don't obey, things happen.

And they're usually not good things.

Because Cain didn't obey God when it came to the right way to worship, there were consequences. Cain became angry and discouraged when God rejected his offering. You know what happens when you get upset. You feel all the bad emotions, and you react by screaming or stomping off or crying.

Cain's mistake—not worshipping God the right way—affected his emotions. His cheap worship produced cheap results, and bad stuff happened as a result.

BE A HERO, NOT A VILLAIN

Do you remember what the opposite of a hero is? A villain. The bad guy. The one who never wins in the end.

Sin makes you a villain. When sin takes over your life, you make bad choices. Like arguing with your parents. Or yelling at your siblings. Or being mean to a friend. Or putting off doing your homework. Or eating too much sugar. Or never cleaning your messy room. These bad choices can become bad habits, and pretty soon you've forgotten how to get along with others or do your homework right away or eat healthy snacks.

Messed-up emotions can lead to messed-up actions, which can lead to a messed-up life. Which is why it's so important to stay plugged in to God.

If you stay close to God—by praying and reading your Bible and hanging out with other people who follow Him—you can avoid being controlled by sin. When you let God help you control your emotions, He will also help you control your actions. (That's because actions usually follow emotions!)

Now we come to the really bad part of the Cain and Abel story—the part where Cain kills Abel. Because Cain was mad at God, he killed his brother, who had earned God's favor and pleasure by doing the right thing. Jealousy led to first-degree murder (Genesis 4:8). Cain may have thought he would get away with it, but he was wrong. God called him out on his actions.

> The LORD said to Cain, "Where is your brother Abel?"
>
> "I don't know," he replied. "Am I my brother's keeper?"
>
> The LORD said, "What have you done? Listen! Your brother's blood cries out to me from the ground. Now you are under a curse and driven from the ground, which opened its mouth to receive your brother's blood from your hand. When you work the ground, it will no longer yield its crops for you. You will be a restless wanderer on the earth" (Genesis 4:9-12).

This story is very sad, but it's a reminder that God judges the sins that destroy the lives of others. God is good, and He will look out for His children. And in the end, God's side always, always wins.

Living by faith as a kingdom hero means totally trusting God. It means doing what He says you should do, not doing what you feel like doing. (Sometimes this can be hard to figure out. When that happens, ask a parent or grandparent or someone else you trust! You can also ask that person to pray with you.) It means basing your whole life on what God says is true.

THE THREE T'S

Time. Talents. Treasures. Let's call these the three *T*'s.

Write down what you think your time, talents, and treasures are. (When you consider time, think about things you spend too much time on—like watching shows or looking at stuff on your phone. You probably have more time than you think you do!)_____

_____

_____

_____

_____

_____

_____

_____

_____

_____

Time involves what you do and when you do it. Do you play video games or watch shows every day but forget to read your Bible? Do you text your friends a lot but never pray for them? Do you spend tons of time working on your own stuff—even good stuff like doing artwork or making crafts—instead of helping out around the house? God wants you to spend your time connecting with Him and also doing things for others. Love God, love people. Those are the two main commandments Jesus gave us! Spend your *time* doing these things.

Talents are the things you're good at, the things that are fun and come fairly easily to you. We tend to think of a talent as something that can be *performed*—like being good at music or sports or art. But so many things can be considered a talent! Being a good listener is a talent. Taking care of animals is a talent. Encouraging others with kind words and a big smile is a talent. Making friends easily is a talent. Use the talents you have to do good things, and keep trying new things and developing other talents. You never know what God will use in your life!

Treasures can be a little hard to define, but think about these creatively. When you hear the word *treasures*, you might think of things like a big house, a lot of money, or a closet full of expensive clothes and shoes. And God *can* use these things. You can invite others over to your big house for a Bible study. You can give your money to people and groups who need it. You can even share your clothes and shoes with others. But treasures don't always have to do with being wealthy. Maybe you live in a small house, but your dad bakes the best cookies. Those cookies are treasures you can share with your friends. Or you live with your grandparents, and they tell the best stories. Those stories are treasures, for sure! Hunt for the treasures in your life. God has placed them there, and they might not be as hidden as you think.

Are you giving God the time, talents, and treasures He seeks from you? Are you giving Him the first fruits—the very best—of your energy, thoughts, heart, and soul? Or are you just tossing Him some Froot Loops here and there?

You know, the interesting thing about Froot Loops is that even though they come in a bunch of different colors, they all taste the same. No matter what color it is, every piece has the same flavor because they're all made from the same stuff.

It doesn't matter what kind of worship you toss to God or what fancy "color" it is. If it's not what He requires, it all tastes the same to Him. But if you give Him the proper kind of worship, you'll have what it takes to be a kingdom hero. You'll be able to control your emotions. You'll know how to make good decisions. You'll understand what God wants you to say and do.

Who do you want to be? It's up to you. You get to choose whether you'll live as a kingdom hero, a villain, or an extra in this drama called life.

I'm assuming you chose the role of *hero*, so let's get to know some more of those!

2

ENOCH

Walking with God

Faith is measured by your feet, not by your feelings.

What exactly does that mean?

It means that what you *do* is way more important than what you *say* you're going to do. One of the very best ways to see if you really have as much faith as you think you do is to observe how you respond—what you say and what you do—when things go wrong. When you fail a test at school. When your football season ends with a broken arm. When your best friend decides she's found a new best friend.

When these things happen, what do you say? What do you do? Your answers to those two questions will reveal how much faith you have.

When everything goes totally sideways, you will discover what you're truly made of. And you will learn how strong your faith really is. Anyone can look and talk a good faith game. You can wear a cross necklace or talk about going to church or slap some Jesus stickers on your water bottle. (And by the way, there's nothing wrong with doing those things!)

But being a kingdom hero isn't about how you talk. It's about how you *walk*.

A HERO WHO WALKED WITH GOD

I wouldn't be surprised if you've never heard of this next hero we're going to talk about. His name is Enoch, and he's a mystery man to most of us. The Bible doesn't say much about him, but what it *does* say is pretty significant.

Enoch lived a very long time—365 years! And during those 365 years, he did his best to live a righteous life and obey God. Genesis 5:24 says, "Enoch walked faithfully with God; then he was no more, because God took him away."

How you walk—and whom you walk with—matters. Enoch walked *faithfully*. And he walked *with God*. If you walk faithfully with God, you will stay close enough to Him to have full access to His wisdom, His guidance, and His hand on your life. And you can experience amazing things on this earth! For example, because Enoch walked faithfully with God, he was given the gift of avoiding death.

Walk faithfully. *Walk* with God.

That's right—Enoch never died. He just went from walking with God on earth to walking with Him in heaven. It sounds crazy, but it's true. And we know it's true because the Bible says it happened: "By faith Enoch was taken from this life, so that he did not experience death: 'He could not be found, because God had taken him away'" (Hebrews 11:5).

God was pleased with him, so He just took Enoch away. It was the natural next step for Enoch to keep walking with God right up to the gates of heaven—and through them. What an incredible experience!

YOUR OWN WALK

Enoch and God were super close. But keep in mind that in their walk together, it was Enoch walking with God and not God walking with Enoch. That's important to remember, because most people want *God* to walk with *them.* They say, *This is where I'm going, God, and You can join me.* But that's not how it works. If you want to be a kingdom hero, you need to walk where God is going. He knows where to go. You don't.

You follow Him. He doesn't follow you.

You ask Him what He wants you to do and where He wants you to go.

You walk with God.

The Bible tells us to walk by the Spirit (Galatians 5:16). When you walk by the Spirit, you're walking in step with God's leading. You take step after step based on His Word. You don't skip any steps by hopping, skipping, or jumping over them. You *walk.* That means it's an ongoing action that you keep doing—over and over and over again.

When you choose to walk with God, you choose to have Him right there by your side. And this is a very good thing! God can help you make good decisions. He can help you know what to say and what to do when you're completely confused. When you walk with God, you don't have Him join you for only part of your day—like your once-a-week piano lesson or your Saturday morning soccer game. You walk with Him *all* the time!

What are some situations in your own life where you need to start walking with God? Write them down here. You can even draw a picture of yourself walking with God. _____

_____

_____

_____

_____

_____

_____

_____

_____

_____

_____

_____

INTENTION, NOT PERFECTION

Walking with God as a kingdom hero doesn't require you to be perfect. It just requires you to be *intentional*—or trying your best.

Take Isaac, for example. He had a problem with lying. In fact, he even lied about his own wife, Rebekah, at one point, saying she was his sister! The Bible says that Isaac lied because he was afraid and selfish:

> When the men of that place asked him about his wife, he said, "She is my sister," because he was afraid to say, "She is my wife." He thought, "The men of this place might kill me on account of Rebekah, because she is beautiful" (Genesis 26:7).

Then there's Jacob. As a father, he was known for being a deceiver, manipulator, and overall bad dude. After all, he raised up sons who would sell their younger brother, Joseph, into slavery. Jacob was messed up. (You can read about some of Jacob's trickery in Genesis 25:19-34 and Genesis 27–28:5.)

But both Isaac and Jacob were kingdom heroes! That's because despite their failures, they chose to turn their hearts back to God, have faith in Him, and walk with Him. They weren't perfect, but they were *intentional* about following God.

This is good news! God is the God of second chances. Or third chances. Or however many chances it takes to get it right. He always gives you the chance to make up for the mess-ups in your past. And He always gives you more chances to create a better tomorrow!

SOMETIMES IT RAINS

Not too long ago I took part in an outdoor photo shoot. Unfortunately, it rained that day. And everyone was too busy to reschedule it. So there we were, taking pictures in the rain. In fact, it poured during parts of the photo shoot—a storm complete with the loudest thunder I'd heard in a long time.

We tried to get creative and stay out of the rain, but it was impossible. Needless to say, I didn't manage to stay dry, even with an umbrella. This was because I was surrounded by water.

If you walk in the rain, you experience the effects of the rain. In short, you get wet!

If you walk with God, you experience the effects of God. He's a part of every aspect of your life. Every decision. Every thought. Every dream. Everything!

I'm sure you've gone for a walk with a friend or family member. And I'm guessing that person is someone you like. (Well, maybe you don't like your brother or sister *all* the time, but mostly you do, right?) When you walk with someone, you spend time with them. You match your pace so you can walk together. You talk with them. Sometimes you even just walk together in the quiet and notice all the pretty trees and grass and flowers all around you.

Amos 3:3 says, "Do two walk together unless they have agreed to do so?" It's hard to go for a walk when you're fighting with someone. But when you're getting along with them, walking together is fun and relaxing.

Go for a walk with someone. Make it a fun experience. Bring your puppy. Go get ice cream. Take some pictures. Most of all, have fun walking and talking together! Where did you go? What did you do?

_____

_____

_____

_____

_____

_____

_____

_____

If you're disagreeing with someone about anything at all, it will be hard to walk in step with them. It will be hard to hang out together, simply because you're not on the same page. You're not walking together if you're on two different sides of the street.

When you choose to walk with God, you've decided you want to walk with Him on the same side of the street. You want His influence in your life. You want to agree with Him. And you're ready to follow where He leads you.

GET CLOSE TO GOD

You can take your dog for a walk, but you can't really walk *with* your dog because you're not totally on the same page. You can't turn to your dog and say, "Fido, what do you think about this?" and expect to get a helpful answer. Your dog can't respond with much more than a bark, whine, or growl. You can take a guess at what each of those dog noises means, but you'll never know for sure. Why? Because you're not the same.

But with God, you *can* exchange information in a way that is understood by both sides. God understands everything that's going through your mind. He knows how you feel when you're sad, happy, or scared. He really and truly *gets* you.

This next part is super important.

> *When you walk with God, you need*
> *to believe that God is really there.*

Now, this might sound totally obvious, but sometimes we forget. And it's hard to walk with someone if you're unsure they're even there. Hebrews 11:6 says, "Without faith it is impossible to please God, because anyone who comes to him must believe that he exists and that he rewards those who earnestly seek him."

If you doubt that God is even there, how can you hear from Him? When you can't physically see someone, it's hard to know they are there. But God promises you that He is always right there with you.

Some people think of God as just floating around somewhere out there in the universe. He's big enough and wise enough to hang the stars and create the world, but that's as close as He gets. This isn't true, though. God is the Creator, but He's also more than that. He is knowable. He is relatable. He has emotions. And He wants to hang out with you and me every day. He wants to show us what to do and say. He wants to direct us where to go. And He wants to help us make good decisions so our lives please Him and bring us peace and purpose.

Write down everything you do in a day, including the time of day you do them. Now, circle the times when God is with you. (You can circle *everything* because God is with you 100 percent of the time!)

_____

_____

_____

_____

_____

_____

_____

_____

_____

_____

_____

_____

If your parents are divorced or if you have friends whose parents are divorced, you probably know all about custody and visitation rights. Some kids live with their mom during the week and with their dad on the weekends. Or they go back and forth between their parents' houses. They're not with both their mom and dad 100 percent of the time.

You can be with God 100 percent of the time, though. You're not just with Him in church. Or only on Sundays or when you're praying. He's always there. You just need to believe and have faith that He's always with you.

KINGDOM HERO SPOTLIGHT
David

David was young when God chose him. He was short. He was small. Yet none of this mattered when he went up against a giant named Goliath.

In 1 Samuel 17, we read about how David grabbed a slingshot and five smooth stones to go after his enemy. Let me tell you, David was such a great shot that it only took one stone to bring the bully down.

David never let the size of the battle determine where it wound up. He overcame all odds because of his great faith and heart after God. With God on your side, you're never outmatched.

BELIEVING IN WHAT YOU DON'T SEE

Once there was a teacher who didn't believe in God. She asked her students if they could see the trees outside the window.

One of the kids answered, "Yes, I see the trees."

Then she asked, "Can you see the flowers?" The kids nodded yes.

"What about the sky?" she asked. "Who can see the sky?"

"I can," each kid answered as they raised their hands.

The teacher lowered her voice. "Can you see God?"

One of the kids in the front row answered, "No, I can't see God."

"Then He must not exist," she responded.

"Wait," the kid said. "Can I ask you a question?" When the teacher nodded, the student asked, "Can you see your brain?"

Laughing, she said, "No, I can't see my brain."

"Then it must not exist!" the wise child responded, and the entire class erupted in laughter.

You and I believe in many things we don't see. Just because we can't see God doesn't mean He's not there. We can see evidence of Him all around us—in the trees and the flowers and the sky. Not being able to see God physically shouldn't keep us from believing He exists.

The first part of walking with God is believing that He exists and that He wants to have a relationship with us. The second part, according to Hebrews 11:6, is believing that He rewards those of us who seek Him.

That's what the kingdom hero Enoch did. He believed in God. And he decided to seek Him. Enoch chose to spend time in God's presence, walking with Him.

Enoch had been walking with God for so long and so closely that God eventually just took him home alive. After 300 years of walking closely together, God probably said something like, "Hey, Enoch, let's just keep on going." They were closer to heaven by that point anyhow, so I imagine the two of them just kept walking until they got there.

What God did with Enoch—walking with him all the way to heaven—could for sure be considered a miracle. And while God probably won't do the exact same thing with you, He can still make miracles happen in your life.

When you're really scared of something and God takes away your fear, that's a miracle.

When God helps you through a bad situation, that's a miracle.

When you're totally unsure of what to do but God provides a path and you take it, that's a miracle.

YOUR PERSONAL GPS

Write down the directions from your house to your best friend's house. How much can you remember? Giving directions can be hard—especially if you're not used to paying attention to where you're going!

_____

_____

_____

_____

_____

_____

_____

_____

_____

_____

Anyone who knows me knows that when it comes to technology, I have a long way to go. One time I got behind the wheel of my car like normal, with the directions printed on paper like normal, only to have everyone else in the car look at me as if I were crazy.

"What are you doing?" one of my passengers asked me with a look of shock.

"I'm reading the directions," I responded.

He looked at my hand holding the piece of paper and at my other hand on the wheel. He then looked at the screen in the middle of my console, which was dark. "You do know you have a GPS that will tell you where to go, right?" he asked. "You don't need that paper anymore." Then he started pushing some buttons on the screen. Once he'd finished, a map appeared on the screen and a voice I'd never heard spoke through my car speakers, telling me where to go.

"See, you are the arrow," my passenger explained, pointing to the screen. "Your arrow will follow this line while you keep listening to the invisible person, and she'll also guide you if you need additional help."

The GPS and the invisible person did help us get to our location a lot easier than if I'd just used my paper. But I had to be willing to learn to use something I wasn't used to using.

You may not be used to hearing the voice of God. You may not be used to walking with Him. And it might be hard to start including Him in everything in your life all day, all week, all year long. You may even forget to ask for His help when things get hard. But if you'll use this tool God has given you—walking with Him—and learn how to use it, you'll get to where you're going faster and easier. God will lead you where you need to go. All you need to do is follow His direction.

If you choose not to listen to God's GPS, you're going to wind up tuning into someone else's GPS. No matter what, someone or something will guide you. You get to choose who or what that guide is. But you need to choose wisely. And remember this:

Kingdom heroes always choose God.

Now, God's specific directions for you may not be the same today as they were yesterday. God may give you different directions on different days. Maybe one day, His best choice is for you to ignore the kid who always makes mean comments. But on another day, maybe God wants you to talk to that kid and find out what's really going on with him. Maybe God has been working in his life, and now the timing is right for the two of you to talk. And maybe even talk about God. You just never know!

God never changes, but His methods often do. That's why it's important to stay closely connected to Him and follow the directions He gives you.

KNOWN BY GOD

It might surprise you to learn that the kingdom hero Enoch was not well known or recognized by others who lived when he lived. He wasn't famous. He had no amazing reputation. He wasn't a big name. He didn't even have a burial! But he was known by God. He walked with God. And when the time came for him to leave this earth and head into heaven, he walked there with God as well.

Who do you want to be?

Do you want to be an earthly hero who's here today and gone tomorrow?

Or do you want to be a kingdom hero who draws the attention of angels and is known by God Himself?

You get to choose. You can live for other people and be well known here on this earth, or you can live for God and be well known one day in heaven.

Popularity doesn't last. People may know you today but not tomorrow.

I learned this firsthand when my wife and I went to Israel with our ministry a few years ago. Three of our kids were also on the trip, including my daughter, Priscilla Shirer. Most everyone I run into now knows who Priscilla is because she had roles in the blockbuster films *War Room* and *I Can Only Imagine*. She's also a super popular Christian speaker. (I'm sure your mom knows who Priscilla is!)

When Priscilla and I were filming a portion of our Bible study at the garden of Gethsemane, we were suddenly swarmed by a group of women from a tour bus. They wanted to have their picture taken with… Priscilla. People often recognize me, but I stood off to the side as everyone rushed up to my daughter to grab a photo with her. I smiled because Priscilla used to stand off to the side so people could greet me. Now it's the other way around!

People from one "tour bus" may know you, but then the next one pulls up, and those people push you out of the way to get to someone else!

If you're a kingdom hero, you don't need to worry about popularity here on earth. No matter how famous you are, someone else will always be more famous. No matter how many friends you have, someone else will always have more friends. No matter how many followers you have on social media, someone else will always have more followers.

Don't compare! And don't worry. Just be like Enoch. Walk with God and let Him do His thing in your life.

Because being a kingdom hero isn't about how you *talk*. It's about how you *walk*.

3

NOAH

Activating Your Faith

Have you ever gotten a plant or tried to grow some flowers? At first, you're really careful to water the plant or your flower seeds. But then a week goes by. Or maybe two weeks. You forget to water. And you know what happens? The soil dries up. The plant withers and dies. The seeds never sprout because they don't have enough water to grow.

The same thing can happen with faith. It can dry up. It dries up when you forget to nurture it, when you forget to pray and read your Bible and connect with other Christians. It dries up when you forget to hang out with Jesus.

ACTIVATE YOUR FAITH!

When you play a video game, your goal is to get to the next level, right? It's the same way with faith. There's always another level you can get to. And each level draws you closer to God. The Bible explains it this way:

What good is it, my brothers and sisters, if someone claims to have faith but has no deeds? Can such faith save them? Suppose a brother or sister is without clothes or daily food. If one of you says to them, "Go in peace; keep warm and well fed," but does nothing about their physical needs, what good is it? In the same way, faith by itself, if it is not accompanied by action, is dead (James 2:14-17).

Faith that doesn't do anything isn't really faith. It isn't active. It doesn't work. It doesn't get us to the next level. But we can always reactivate our faith by making sure our actions match our beliefs. We believe that God loves us and wants us to love others, so we do something about it! We help a friend clean her room. We quiz our little sister on her spelling words. We collect warm coats for kids in need. Actions bring faith to life!

> *If you believe something is*
> *true, you need to act on it.*

Just think about what would have happened if Noah had waited for everyone to agree with him that building the ark was a good idea. (Pretty much everyone said he was stupid for building it!) None of us would be here today. The ark never would have gotten built! When the flood came, the entire population would have been wiped out. Game over.

Thankfully, though, Noah's faith had been activated. His faith showed up in what he did—building an ark. It wasn't just about what he said or how he felt. He believed that what God was telling him was true, and then he acted on it. He did something. He did something big. He built an ark.

If you feel like your faith isn't super strong, it's time to reactivate it! What actions can you take to make your faith strong again?

_____

_____

_____

_____

_____

_____

_____

_____

_____

_____

NOAH'S SECRET

Hebrews 11:7 says, "By faith Noah, when warned about things not yet seen, in holy fear built an ark to save his family. By his faith he condemned the world and became heir of the righteousness that is in keeping with faith."

Noah's story is a perfect example of faith at work. He didn't care what others thought about him. He didn't care that others were calling him crazy. He didn't care about being popular. He only cared what God thought—and he did what God asked him to do.

It's really hard not to care what others think of us. What was Noah's secret? His secret was that *he lived to please God.* He walked with God, and doing what God wanted him to do was always his top priority. More than having a bunch of friends. More than having others think of him as successful. More than becoming famous or well known.

Most of us know the story of Noah and the ark from our earliest Sunday school lessons. Even nonbelievers have heard of Noah's ark. Building a huge boat was quite a task, but Noah's walk of faith and actions of obedience were even more amazing because of the world in which Noah lived. Nobody else around him was walking with God. Talk about peer pressure! In fact, people were doing such bad things that God was going to send a flood, wipe everyone out, and start over again. Yikes!

But because Noah and his family were following God, they were saved. They just needed to do what God asked them to do. Even if it went against what everyone else was doing.

Write about a time when you've felt like you were the only one doing what God wanted you to do. To make things easier for you the next time you're in a similar situation, write down a plan for sticking close to God and following His directions. _____

_____

_____

_____

_____

_____

_____

_____

_____

_____

_____

_____

_____

_____

_____

WHAT HAPPENS WHEN YOU IGNORE SIN

What happens when you don't clean something up? It gets worse, right? For example, if you were to leave some old food in your backpack, it would get super moldy and gross. Pretty soon it would start attracting some flies and who knows what else. And the smell when you unzipped your messy backpack? Nasty!

Gross things spread. And sin is a gross thing, so sin spreads.

That's why it's so important to keep your heart, mind, and life clean. Just as it's important to take the trash and food out of your backpack, it's important to take the trash of sin out of your life. You do this by staying connected to God. He helps you understand what's right and what's wrong and what you need to talk to Him about and ask forgiveness for.

Ignoring sin is about as smart as letting all your leftover lunches pile up in your backpack. Can you imagine what that would look like and smell like after a week? How about a month? Disgusting! When we allow the sin in our lives to go unaddressed, we create a gross environment where bad stuff multiplies. And the longer you let it go, the harder it is to clean.

BIG FAITH

Many of us are waiting on God, but the fact is, God is often waiting on us. Sure, we may be praying, but praying is just one part of faith. Faith also requires footsteps. Faith requires action.

One day, when the Israelites were trying to escape from the Egyptian army, they came to a dead end. Their path was blocked by the Red Sea. God instructed Moses to lift his rod to part the huge body of water. God performed a double miracle that day. First, He held back the waters. And second, He dried the muddy, wet ground and made it firm enough for the Israelites, their wagons, and their animals to cross. Everyone traveled safely through the sea bed because God hardened the ground beneath them. What's more, once the Israelites had safely passed through, God lured the Egyptians onto the same path, only to close the waters over them.

> Then the LORD said to Moses, "Stretch out your hand over the sea so that the waters may flow back over the Egyptians and their chariots and horsemen." Moses stretched out his hand over the sea, and at daybreak the sea went back to its place. The Egyptians were fleeing toward it, and the LORD swept them into the sea. The water flowed back and covered the chariots and horsemen—the entire army of Pharaoh that had followed the Israelites into the sea. Not one of them survived (Exodus 14:26-28).

The Israelites watched as God not only dried the land but also returned the waters to their original place to stop the Egyptians from chasing after them. All of this happened because the Israelites were willing to step out in faith.

If you never step out in faith, you'll never see what God can do. And while it might be easy to obey Him on the little things, it's much harder on the big things. But obey Him anyway! Because God promises to show up and do miraculous things in your life when you have big faith.

BE GOD'S PERSON

Your friends might be pressuring you to do certain things or to act a certain way. And you know God would be disappointed in you if you did those things or acted that way. Even social media puts a lot of pressure on you to imitate certain thoughts, words, or actions. This pressure can be super stressful. It can squeeze you tighter and tighter until you feel like you're going to burst. And it's really tempting to just give in so you can blend in with everyone else.

Most of us find that it's easy to be a Christian in church. There, everyone pretty much agrees on the main things. Jesus loves us. God wants us to follow Him. Some things are right and some things are wrong. But when you go out into the world—school, your activities, a friend's house, or the online world—the pressure to be like everyone else builds. And that pressure can become dangerous.

Write down some things that are important to kids your age, like clothes, music, social media, and so on. How important are these things to God? Pray and ask God to help you focus on the things *He* says are important. _____

_____

_____

_____

_____

_____

_____

_____

_____

_____

When you walk closely with God, He won't let the pressure get to you. His presence will keep you from worrying about what everyone else thinks. You'll be so busy walking with God and hanging out with Him that you won't care what you're missing out on. Because you're in the best place possible and doing the best thing possible!

Kingdom heroes stay
focused on God, not others.

LISTEN TO GOD

Noah didn't give in to the world's pressure. He lived a good life when everyone around him was doing some really bad stuff. He walked with God. As a result, God saved Noah and his family from the flood. In fact, in Hebrews 11:7 we see that God even warned Noah ahead of time so he could prepare for what was going to happen. He gave Noah a sneak peek of the situation that was about to unfold.

Wouldn't it be nice if we could know what is going to happen in the future? It would sure help us make decisions or not worry about things! And it would make life a lot less stressful if we could prepare for things because we knew ahead of time that they were going to happen. Noah was able to have enough time to plan what he was going to do because God had warned him ahead of time of the disaster that was about to happen. And He gave Noah some beyond-helpful advice: Build an ark!

Listening to God makes life a whole lot easier. You hear His voice when you're tuned in to Him. You tune in to Him by praying, reading your Bible, going to church, and listening to more mature Christians. All those things will help you sort out what God is saying and how that's different from what the world is saying.

Noah heard the voice of God, and he took what God said to heart. He got busy. He followed God's direction:

> So God said to Noah, "I am going to put an end to all people, for the earth is filled with violence because of them. I am surely going to destroy both them and the earth. So make yourself an ark of cypress wood; make rooms in it and coat it with pitch inside and out" (Genesis 6:13-14).

KINGDOM HERO SPOTLIGHT

Gideon (Judges 6–7)

Gideon was a leader, but he was a scared leader. He was not very brave sometimes. But God called on him because Israel was being invaded by the enemy, and He needed Gideon to do something about it. Even though Gideon was afraid, he pulled together an army of 32,000 men.

But then God told him he had too many men.

Gideon was confused. How could 32,000 men be too many when going up against a much larger enormous army? But God knew better. He asked Gideon to shrink his army to just 300 men. At this point, Gideon must have felt lost. How could he win a battle against tens of thousands when he had just 300 men? But that's when God reminded him it wasn't just 300 men. It was 300 men plus God. The "plus God" part would make the difference. So Gideon let go of his own battle plans and chose to trust God.

Obeying God, Gideon ended up winning the battle with just 300 men. We should always do what God asks us to do, even when we can't understand how something will work. It's by faith that Gideon's army of 300 won—and it's by faith that we will win too.

JUST DO IT—ALL OF IT

God gave Noah detailed instructions for how to build a big boat that would hold up in weather the world had never seen: rain. (Yep, you read that right—Noah had never seen rain!) Once he had received the instructions, Noah got to work. He set out to do what had never been done. He'd never even seen a flood. Up to this point, the earth had received water only one way—out of the ground. And Noah lived 100 miles away from an ocean. He didn't have a truck or a trailer to haul the ark to deep water once it was built. But none of that stopped Noah. He just did it—all of it. Everything God had asked him to do.

I'm sure Noah's neighbors were totally talking about him and throwing him under the bus. And I'm sure that happened more and more as Noah's ark got bigger and bigger. "What does this dude think he's doing?" everyone must have been saying.

But that's what you can expect to happen when you walk so close to God that He tells you His secrets.

When God speaks to you about what He plans to do, and He asks you to take part in it, what He asks of you will often appear weird to the world. Like loving your mean neighbor. Or giving your possessions to the poor. Or going to church instead of sleeping in on Sunday mornings. In fact, most of the time, the bigger God's plans are, the weirder they seem to others.

Noah built a boat on dry land—a structure roughly one and a half football fields long and four stories high. And he spent 120 years doing it! Genesis 6:22 says, "Noah did everything just as God commanded him."

That's the definition of a kingdom hero in three words:

Noah did everything.

Every single thing God commanded him to do, Noah did. It was a massive amount of work, but he did all of it.

Noah's story is a reminder to us all: When God asks us to do something, we should do it. All of it. Even if it seems weird. Even if it doesn't quite make sense. Even if others make fun of us for doing it. Obedience is the key to activating our faith as kingdom heroes. People who walk by faith do everything God tells them to do—not just some of it.

WALK YOUR TALK

Noah's actions spoke louder than his words, and his entire life gives us a good example of what it means to follow God and walk with Him. Even though he didn't know how all the animals would get on the boat or how the boat would find its way to water, Noah did what he could, right where he was, with what he had—because that's what God told him to do. He didn't have to know everything ahead of time. He just needed to know that God would take care of him.

The message here is super simple:

Just do what God says to do.

When it's time to bring about a miracle or a heroic move, God will be right there. He won't be late. He's prepared. And you just need to do what He says to do. That's it! That's the key to activating your faith.

GET GOING!

You may wonder, *Why don't we see God at work in our lives more often?* Often, the answer is that our feet aren't moving, or if they are, they're moving slowly, partially, or in the wrong direction.

I completely understand that life can be hard. And following God's path isn't always easy. Maybe kids make fun of you for believing in Jesus. Maybe obeying your parents is really, really hard—especially when you see your friends disobeying their parents. Maybe standing up for the classmate who's being bullied makes you a target, so you're scared to do anything. But whatever your situation may be, a day will come when God will make clear to everyone just where He stands. And if your feet are moving in step with His, you'll find yourself safe in His camp. Which, in the end, is the only place you want to be.

Noah walked in step with God. He made his decisions based on what he knew about the future so that when the bad stuff happened, he was well prepared for whatever life threw at him. His faith was activated, and he was ready.

We can't know exactly what is going to happen in the future, but God tells us that what we do today can make our tomorrow better. When we choose to walk closely with God and do what He asks us to do, we'll be kingdom heroes who are ready and prepared to handle anything.

Keep nurturing your faith. Keep listening to God. Keep staying connected to Him. Keep praying and reading your Bible and hanging out with other friends who love Jesus. As a kingdom hero, it's important to take actions that activate your faith!

4

ABRAHAM

Passing the Test

There are two ways you can live your life.

One is by *sight*.

The other is by *faith*.

You can live by what you see in the world around you and not pay attention to God. Or you can live by faith and decide to do things (or not do them!) based on what God says.

The choice is up to you.

The next kingdom hero we're going to learn about, Abraham, totally lived by faith. Hebrews 11:8-10 says this about Abraham's life:

> By faith Abraham, when called to go to a place he would later receive as his inheritance, obeyed and went, even though he did not know where he was going. By faith he made his home in the promised land like a stranger in a foreign country; he lived

in tents, as did Isaac and Jacob, who were heirs with him of the same promise. For he was looking forward to the city with foundations, whose architect and builder is God.

Abraham did three things in his kingdom hero journey.
He *left*.
He *lived*.
And he *looked*.

LEAVING

Abraham began his hero's journey by *leaving*. When God told him "Go!" he took off from where he'd been living all his life.

The LORD had said to [Abraham], "Go from your country, your people and your father's household to the land I will show you.

"I will make you into a great nation,
and I will bless you;
I will make your name great,
and you will be a blessing.
I will bless those who bless you,
and whoever curses you I will curse;
and all peoples on earth
will be blessed through you."

So [Abraham] went, as the LORD had told him; and Lot went with him. [Abraham] was seventy-five years old when he set out from Harran (Genesis 12:1-4).

When you think of a hero setting out to do something big, you don't think of a 75-year-old, do you? But that's how old Abraham was when he set out on his kingdom hero journey!

Abraham's situation was a little like Noah's. More than a little, actually. Both men lived at a time when everyone around them was doing some really bad stuff and not listening to God. During Abraham's time, a man named Nimrod had led the people to rebel against God. In fact, Nimrod had the Tower of Babel built to show that civilization was now human-centered, not God-centered.

God saw that rather than following Him, people were following themselves. Instead of worshipping Him, they were worshipping themselves. In short, the people thought they were better than God.

So God did something about it. He scrambled up their language so they couldn't understand each other. And He also "scattered them… over all the earth" (Genesis 11:8). This is what got Abraham moving and heading somewhere brand-new. This is what caused Abraham to leave.

God knew that for Abraham to live out his purpose as a kingdom hero, he had to leave everything he'd ever known. But God wasn't going to tell Abraham exactly where He was taking him. Abraham had to trust that God knew where He was taking him. He had to have *faith*.

With a sibling or a friend, take turns blindfolding each other and leading each other around. Is it easy to tell where you're going? Is it hard to have total trust in your guide?_____

_____

_____

_____

_____

_____

_____

_____

_____

_____

Abraham left the land where he'd been living because he had faith that God had something even better for him. God also has something even better for you. But you can't get there without following Him. If you're following the world and its values, entertainment systems, priorities, and more, you're not following God. And He can't communicate with you when you have the world's "music" blaring all around you.

Has your family ever gone on vacation and stayed at a hotel or an Airbnb or a campsite expecting to have some quiet, chill, family time? Maybe you were planning on filling your days with swimming and naps and reading and eating and just hanging out. But when you got to your destination, you discovered that the people next to you were super loud. They turned their terrible music way up, or they yelled and fought the whole time. It changed the whole vacation! Suddenly you were spending all your time trying to escape your obnoxious neighbors.

Needing to escape the noise of the world isn't anything new. Even Jesus went away to a quiet place when He needed to talk with His Father. Sometimes you need to put yourself in a place where the only voice you hear is God's.

EVEN WHEN THINGS ARE GOOD

It might surprise you to learn that Abraham's life wasn't that bad when God called him to leave. Actually, things were going just fine! Abraham wasn't sad. He wasn't poor. He wasn't lonely. He had friends. He had money. He had success. Everyone knew him and liked him. It probably wasn't easy for him to drop everything and move on. But that's what God called him to do, so he did it.

Kingdom heroes always know that the new thing God has for them is better than what they currently have. They grab on to God's hand and go where He's going.

When I was a kid, I used to spend hours playing marbles. Back then, marbles were the "in" thing to do, and over time, I got very good at the game. In fact, one time I was six feet back from the center and aimed my marble so accurately that when I hit the marble I was going for, it cracked the marble in half!

Playing marbles was super fun. But when I became a teenager, something happened. Someone handed me a football, and suddenly I was way more into football than marbles. I played more and more football and less and less marbles until I stopped playing marbles altogether. My new direction had taken me to a new place.

Sometimes when we're handed something new, we don't try it out. We stick with what we know. And we miss out on what could have been. If I had stuck with marbles and didn't try football, I would have missed out on all the fun and joy that football has brought me.

If you stick with what your friends want you to do instead of what God wants you to do, you're going to miss out on some great stuff. God knows where He wants to take you, but you must be willing to leave, step out in faith, and follow Him.

That might mean you stop hanging out with friends who don't love Jesus and pressure you to do things you're not comfortable doing. It might mean giving up one activity so you can focus on another because that's what you feel God leading you to do. It might mean deleting your social media account because you spend way too much time on it.

What might be holding you back from going where God wants you to go? Write your ideas down here, and then pray that God will make clear where He wants to take you. _____

_____

_____

_____

_____

_____

_____

_____

_____

_____

_____

_____

Do you want to live out God's plan for you? Or do you want the world's plan? You get to choose. In fact, you *have* to choose because you can't have both.

If you want to live a kingdom hero's life
of faith, you need to choose God's plan.

THE WAITING GAME

Do you know the feeling of being close but not quite close enough? You're almost old enough to go to the fun session of summer camp—the one where you can do the zip line and ride horses and paddle the canoes without a counselor in the boat—but your birthday happens to fall the week *after* camp. Or you're almost good enough for the choir solo, but someone else is just a little bit better. So you have to wait to try out for the solo another year, which feels like forever.

Sometimes it can feel harder to wait for something when you're so close to it! If what you're waiting for is super far off in the distance—like getting your driver's license or going away to college—it's not so hard. You have so much to do in between, and it just seems so far off. But when it's close—like a birthday or summer vacation or a sleepover at your best friend's house—waiting can be really, really hard.

When you're waiting for something, God is doing two things in your life. First, He's *preparing the promise for you.* And second, He's *preparing you for the promise.*

God prepares the promise *for* you.
And He prepares you *for the* promise.

These might sound like the same thing, but they're not.

Think about your parents giving you a surprise—like a trip to Disneyland or a new clarinet. First, they have to get the surprise ready. They have to buy the tickets and book the hotel, or they have to save up money for the instrument. And then they have to get you ready for the surprise. They have to make sure to schedule the trip for when you can miss school or be certain that clarinet is really your *thing* and that you'll have plenty of opportunities to practice and play it.

God did the same thing with Abraham. Before God gave him what He had planned for him, Abraham first needed to spend some time waiting—growing in his faith, trusting in God fully—even when it didn't look like anything was going to happen.

KEEP YOUR FEET MOVING

God doesn't want any of us to get too attached to the world we live in. He doesn't want us to get our feet stuck where we are. If we keep our feet moving, that frees us up to walk more freely with God. And He wants to take us on some long and winding paths. Staying tied too closely to your comfort zone will totally limit what God is able to do in your life.

When I stay in a hotel, I don't unpack my suitcase or put my clothes away in the drawers. I don't hang pictures of my family on the walls. I don't organize my stuff in the bathroom. That's because I'm just passing through. I don't plan to stay there much longer than one or two nights. I don't take over the hotel room as if I lived there, simply because I know I'm not staying.

If you want God to take you places, keep your bags packed and your shoes on and your feet moving, because you're about to go through some stuff. You'll encounter mountains to climb, valleys to go through, hills to hike, and waters to wade through before all is said and done. You'll be on an adventure with God!

By faith Abraham went through the learning curves of life. By faith he made mistakes and grew in wisdom. He was willing to wait on God to prepare the adventure for him and to prepare him for the adventure.

WHERE DO YOU LOOK?

Abraham wanted to live as a kingdom hero. But he wasn't perfect. And he didn't always do the right thing. Yet when he was knocked down, he always got back up and started over. When God told him to pitch his tent in a new location, Abraham didn't pitch a fit. Why? Because he had his eye on the prize. He set his sights on high. He was looking for "the city with foundations, whose architect and builder is God" (Hebrews 11:10).

When you learn to look toward heaven, you'll live better here on earth. But if you stop looking toward heaven and focus only on what's happening on earth, you'll miss out on the rewards of both. This is because here on earth, we can't see clearly. The Bible says, "For now we see only a reflection as in a mirror; then we shall see face to face. Now I know in part; then I shall know fully, even as I am fully known" (1 Corinthians 13:12).

As kingdom heroes, we are to look at life from heaven's perspective. This doesn't mean we give up on everything here on earth. Not at all! But it does mean we bring God's rule, His thoughts, and His words into our own lives here on earth.

WHERE TO LOOK WHEN THINGS GET TOUGH

Do you know anyone who suffers from asthma? Maybe that someone is you.

When my son Anthony was young, he suffered from asthma, and when an attack set in, I sometimes had to take him to the ER. But if I had the opportunity, I would take him to his primary care provider, Dr. Denny. That's because Anthony and I knew Dr. Denny.

As Anthony sat on my lap wheezing or trying to get his breath, Dr. Denny would reach into a drawer and pull out a sucker (or lollipop). Even though Anthony would be struggling to breathe, he would go for the candy every single time. As he licked it, Dr. Denny would come around to Anthony's side and give him a shot that would make the asthma attack go away.

At first, the sting in his arm drew Anthony's attention away from his treat, and he would let out a cry. He was not only in pain but also felt faked out by the doctor and betrayed by his dad for taking him to a place where a needle was stuck into his arm. Anthony would look at me with a confused expression, wondering why his father—who said he loved him—would take him to a place of pain.

But it didn't take long for the pain to go away, and Anthony would go back to the sugary candy in his hand. With tears flowing down his face, he started licking that sucker again, and before he knew it, things had changed. He was no longer crying. And he was no longer wheezing. The sweetness of the candy and the healing effect of the medicine had taken hold. He was going to be okay.

We've all felt like Anthony. We've all felt scared. We've all felt betrayed. We've all felt pain. But we also know where to look when things get tough. We look to God.

Where you look determines where you wind up. It's impossible to walk forward if you're looking behind. You can't live out greatness in your future if you're staring at your past. You need to listen when God speaks to you. Leave when He tells you to go. And when you do go, go all-in so you can learn the lessons He has for you.

Keep your eyes on God as He gives you the direction you need to live your life as a kingdom hero. Like Abraham, kingdom heroes don't always know what's around the next corner or over the next hill, but one thing they do know—if they just keep walking with God, they will do incredible things and travel to amazing places!

What do you think God might have for you? It can be hard to know, but start by making a list of things you love—people, places, activities... anything that brings you joy. You can even make an "inspiration board" of images that make you happy and things that remind you of God's love. _____

_____

_____

_____

_____

_____

_____

_____

_____

_____

KINGDOM HERO SPOTLIGHT

Samuel

Samuel struggled a lot in his life. He was a weak father who never talked to his sons when they turned away from God (1 Samuel 8:1-3). Samuel had some major flaws, but when Samuel was willing to operate by faith, God used him to anoint the king of Israel, who would set the nation on a spiritual course toward victory and strength.

TEST TIME

School always comes with tests, doesn't it? When it comes time to figure out what you've learned, your teacher will give you a test. And the results of the test reveal whether you—and your whole class—understand the information that was taught.

Sometimes your teachers give you surprise tests. They might call them "pop quizzes." You're not expecting them, and they can freak you out a little bit. If you forgot to read the chapter and don't know anything, a pop quiz can freak you out a lot!

You also take official, planned tests. Your teacher gives you time to study for these, and they happen on a predictable schedule. Like when you finish the math unit or even a whole school year. These tests cover a lot of material, and passing them means you can move on to the next level.

God gives you tests too. But if you stay connected to Him, you don't have to freak out about these tests. Even if you haven't been talking to Him or reading His Word a lot, He will still help you with the test. You just need to ask.

You can expect a test when God is ready to take you to a new level in your walk with Him. You don't get to move forward just because you want to. First, you need to show that you're ready to move forward.

The bad news is that a test is just that—a test. But the good news is that a test gets you ready for a higher level, which means you have something great to look forward to!

Some tests take forever. Sometimes you have tests back-to-back, in different subjects, and it's hard to keep all the material straight. But whatever the case, God uses these tests to see if you're ready for the next part of your kingdom hero journey.

ABRAHAM'S BIG TEST

The kingdom hero Abraham faced a *super* big test. We read about it in Hebrews 11:17-19:

> By faith Abraham, when God tested him, offered Isaac as a sacrifice. He who had embraced the promises was about to sacrifice his one and only son, even though God had said to him, "It is through Isaac that your offspring will be reckoned." Abraham reasoned that God could even raise the dead, and so in a manner of speaking he did receive Isaac back from death.

Abraham wasn't just facing a pop quiz. This was a major test. God was asking him to sacrifice his son, Isaac. It's a disturbing story, but you'll see that Abraham passes the test—and it all turns out okay.

The really big tests occur when you have to deal with something big in your life. When God is asking you to do something or be something or go somewhere you've never even considered, it's a major exam.

Let's take a look at what God said to Abraham when He gave him this major test:

> Some time later God tested Abraham. He said to him, "Abraham!"

> "Here I am," he replied.

> Then God said, "Take your son, your only son, whom you love—Isaac—and go to the region of Moriah. Sacrifice him there as a burnt offering on a mountain I will show you" (Genesis 22:1-2).

Wow! This makes your end-of-year science test look like no big thing, right? God didn't mince His words in calling Abraham to the table for this test. He very specifically described the type of offering he wanted—a burnt offering. God was letting Abraham know exactly what would be on the test. And that material was enough to scare anybody!

But despite the freaky nature of this test, Abraham went. He obeyed God even though I'm sure he was terrified about how this thing was going to play out. God hadn't even given him any details or any type of test prep. He'd only told Abraham to go, and that when he got there, God would show him what to do next.

Because Abraham was a faithful kingdom hero, he went. He was committed to doing what God had told him to do, even though it didn't make sense. Also, he never thought God would truly let his son die—or he believed that if Isaac did die, God would raise him from the dead. We know this because the Bible says Abraham told this to the men who had come along to carry the wood and supplies for this terrifying test.

WINNER

Most of us have witnessed the excitement of a relay race, seeing competitors run as fast as they can to claim victory. However, as important as each runner's speed is, passing the baton is equally important. No matter how fast the runners are, if they fail to successfully pass the baton, their hard work won't matter. Drop the baton, and you're disqualified. Game over.

Relay races are about *legacy*, or transferring an essential tool to the next person on the journey to reach an agreed-upon destiny and goal.

The baton God has given us to pass is a living, active faith in Him based on His Word, the Bible. When that faith is dropped or not transferred properly, bad things can happen.

The good news, however, is that in His grace, God gives us second chances to pick up the baton of faith and keep going. You can still cross the finish line of life as a winner.

ABRAHAM'S CONFIDENCE

And then there's Abraham's son, Isaac. He must have known something was up when he saw the wood and supplies. But his father was showing only the smallest bit of concern. Abraham even told the men carrying the supplies that both he and Isaac would return after they had finished worshipping.

Abraham had seen God powerfully show up in his life before. That's why he had confidence that God could handle the biggest challenge he'd ever faced. He'd passed yesterday's exams, and he was determined to apply the lessons he'd learned to the current test. He'd learn to trust God despite how things appeared.

Isaac, on the other hand, got nervous—and could you blame him? After all, he and his dad set off to the altar to worship God with everything they needed but the sacrifice itself. Whatever thoughts were racing through Isaac's mind, they didn't take too long to come out in a question: "Father?… The fire and wood are here… but where is the lamb for the burnt offering?" (Genesis 22:7).

Isaac's question didn't fluster Abraham. He just calmly answered, "God himself will provide the lamb for the burnt offering, my son" (verse 8).

Isaac was calmed by his father's words—at least, calmed enough to keep going. He was still probably wondering, but he decided to trust his father, just like Abraham had decided to trust God.

HOW IT ALL TURNED OUT

Isaac must have started to worry more than a little, though, when he found himself on the altar. *Where is that lamb?* he must have been wondering. None of us would have blamed Isaac if he'd said, "Have you lost your mind? What's going on here, Dad?"

Then God spoke to Abraham from heaven: "Do not lay a hand on the boy… Do not do anything to him. Now I know that you fear God, because you have not withheld from me your son, your only son" (Genesis 22:12).

The test was over. Abraham had passed, and Isaac could breathe a sigh of relief.

God will sometimes ask us to sacrifice something that means a lot to us so we can demonstrate our love for Him. It could be a friendship. Or a feeling—like safety or comfort. Or your identity—like being best gymnast on the team or top student in the class or someone without divorced parents. In our lives, things change. You may have to drop out of gymnastics because your mom lost her job and can't afford to pay for your training. Or someone super smart may move into town, and suddenly someone else is getting better grades than you. Or your parents have been fighting and fighting, and they finally break the news that they're getting a divorce.

Write down some times in your own life when you felt like God was testing you. They don't have to be major tests like Abraham's—just times when you felt like you were facing a challenge. What helped you pass the test?_____

_____

_____

_____

_____

_____

_____

_____

_____

_____

_____

_____

_____

_____

_____

_____

_____

_____

But just as God was there for Abraham, God is there for you.

God will help you get through whatever hard situation you face—and pass the test with the best grade possible.

FINISH WHAT YOU'VE BEEN ASKED TO DO

Has your mom or dad ever asked you to clean your room, but you only cleaned up halfway? And you expected them to be happy about it? I mean, you did half the work, right? That's a lot! And they should tell you, "Great job!" Shouldn't they?

Nope. When you're asked to clean your room, you're supposed to clean *all* of it.

It's the same with God. He tells us, *Finish what I've asked you to do.* You aren't called to be a part-time kingdom hero. There's no such thing as a part-time hero anyway. What would happen if Batman chose to answer the bat phone only when he felt like it? He'd miss out on what he needed to do and where he needed to be, and pretty soon he wouldn't be a hero anymore.

Abraham got that. He'd learned that lesson the hard way. But now he'd reached the point where he could pass the major test. And pass it he did. In fact, James 2:21-23 tells us that Abraham not only passed the test with flying colors, but he also got promoted to a unique level—a friend of God.

> Was not our father Abraham considered righteous for what he did when he offered his son Isaac on the altar? You see that his faith and his actions were working together, and his faith was

made complete by what he did. And the scripture was fulfilled that says, "Abraham believed God, and it was credited to him as righteousness," and he was called God's friend.

Now, God loves *everyone*. Each of us is loved by God. But not everyone is known as a friend of God. *Friend* is a special status. Jesus described it like this:

> *"You are my friends if you do what I command"* (John 15:14).

FOCUS ON JESUS

When he was on his way to sacrifice his son, Abraham saw more than just a location in the distance. He saw God's plan. And it made him glad. He smiled. Deep within him, he knew everything he needed to know: The Lord would provide.

Hebrews 12:2 reminds all of us kingdom heroes in training that it's important where we choose to focus and what we choose to focus on. It says we are to be "fixing our eyes on Jesus, the pioneer and perfecter of faith."

While you're on your journey as a kingdom hero, look to Jesus. While you're learning the material that will be on the test, look to Christ. And when you face life's tests, keep in close contact with God. He knows the answers, and He knows everything you'll ever need to know.

5

SARAH

Believing the Impossible

A woman lived far out in the hills of the country. In fact, she lived so far out that her home had no electricity, and she'd been living without it for many years. Then when her area finally got power, the electric company sent somebody to speak to the community's members, telling them about the new power system.

After a few months, the electric company noticed that the woman living far out in the hills barely used any electricity. So they sent a repairman to see if there was a problem with the lines. When he didn't find one, he knocked on the woman's door and asked her if everything was all right.

"Yes, everything's fine," the woman replied. "I use the electricity every single night."

The repairman looked confused, so the woman explained, "I turn on my electric lamp when it's getting dark, so I can see better as I light my kerosene lamp. Then I turn it back off."

The woman had lived without power for so long that she didn't realize she could use her electric lights all the time instead of her old-fashioned kerosene lamps. Instead of using the new power available to her, she just used it briefly and then returned to her old ways.

SARAH'S OLD WAYS

In the Bible, you can read about the kingdom hero Sarah, who had been living in her old ways for a long time. Like a lot of other couples, Sarah and her husband, Abraham, wanted kids. In fact, the Bible promised Abraham and Sarah a child—specifically, a son. Genesis 17:16 says, "I will bless [Sarah] and will surely give [Abraham] a son by her."

Now, the promise of a son doesn't seem like that big a deal. Lots of people have kids, right? Except by then Abraham and Sarah were pretty old. And not just kind of old—Sarah was 90 years old! Many people are great-grandparents by then. Not only was Sarah old, but she'd never given birth to a child. Sarah was pretty sure her dream was *never* going to come true.

All of us know what it's like to have a dream that doesn't work out. Maybe this seems like the year you can finally get straight A's on your report card, but then you fail a math test and the dream disappears. Maybe you're all set to go to the big state gymnastics competition, but then you sprain your ankle and the dream disappears. Maybe this is the first year you will actually have a great group of friends at school, but then you find out you're not in the same class with those friends and the dream disappears.

But don't give up on your dreams! In John 10:10 Jesus promises, "I have come that they may have life, and have it to the full." This means that, even though you might be feeling upset, frustrated, or confused right now, Jesus promises you that it will all work out eventually. And that it will work out better than you could ever imagine!

> What are some dreams you've had that haven't worked out? Don't give up on your dreams! Write them down, and keep praying that God will make them come true in a way that honors Him and gives Him the glory. _____
>
> _____
>
> _____
>
> _____
>
> _____
>
> _____
>
> _____
>
> _____
>
> _____

But back to Sarah and *her* dreams. Five times God had told her that she was going to have a son. Not only that, but He'd gone on to tell both Abraham and Sarah that, through this son, a whole nation would be birthed. Sarah was believing God. She was holding on to God's vision for a great future. Yet she was 90 years old and still no baby. I think most of us would have given up on the dream at that point. Not Sarah, though! She chose to dream big. She chose to keep the faith. She chose to believe the impossible.

Choose to believe the impossible!

MAKE THE TEAM STRONGER

The Bible tells us about something big that happens when we choose to live life as a kingdom hero. This big thing is called your *impact*. Some people call it your *legacy*. Others call it *influence*. Basically, it's how your actions affect others, which can be good or bad, depending on what those actions are.

Kingdom heroes make a *positive impact* on the people around them. They influence and affect others for God's glory and others' good. This is what happened with a group of people—Isaac, Jacob, and Joseph—in Israel's earliest history.

> By faith Isaac blessed Jacob and Esau in regard to their future.
>
> By faith Jacob, when he was dying, blessed each of Joseph's sons, and worshiped as he leaned on the top of his staff (Hebrews 11:20-21).

Isaac, Jacob, and Joseph all passed down a legacy of leadership to those who came after them. They were the best kind of team captains who had a positive impact on the people around them. They weren't in it for their own glory but instead to guide and teach others and to make the team stronger.

KEEPING THE FAITH

Anyone who's waited for anything—and this includes *all* of us—gets what Sarah was going through. You don't want to give up on your dream, but you feel like time is running out. Should you keep hoping for it, or should you forget about the dream and decide to focus on something else?

That's a really hard question.

And that's where being a kingdom hero comes into play—a kingdom hero who keeps the faith despite what the facts might make you think.

For Sarah, the facts were pretty clear. She was 90 years old, and she'd never been able to have kids. Most people would have given up a long time ago. But not Sarah. She was a kingdom hero with *faith*. And she knew that faith is never limited to facts alone. Facts involve what you *see*. Faith involves what you *don't see*.

> Facts involve what you see.
> Faith involves what you don't see.

When facts and faith don't line up, things can get tough. And kind of confusing. God promised you something, but you're not seeing it yet. What's more, you don't see any sign that you will ever get it.

I'm sure Sarah felt her chance at having kids was long gone. Maybe if she were younger, she could still believe in the promise God had given her. But now that she was 90, it was hard to have any faith at all. Maybe she'd heard wrong. Maybe it was all in her imagination. Maybe God had changed His mind and had forgotten to tell her. Maybe it was up to her to do something about it.

DON'T TRY TO HELP GOD

These thoughts and probably more made their home in Sarah's heart, causing her to doubt the promise of having a child. When the promise still hadn't come true after a long period of time, Sarah decided to do what a lot of us decide to do. She decided to "help" God (which of course never works because God doesn't need our help!). And this messed things up.

Sarah decided that if she couldn't have kids, her maid, Hagar, could have kids for her. So she manipulated Hagar into having a child.

God had told Sarah that she would have a child, but then Sarah tried to tell God how this needed to happen. She tried to control the situation and make it happen all by herself, and that's never a good idea. Sarah made her own suggestion for how God's promise could take place because she had stopped having faith that God could fulfill the promise. Basically, Sarah took over.

We can take over too. Sometimes it seems like God is taking too long to do something for us. He's moving too slow. It doesn't seem like there's any way for what He said would happen to happen. We start by thinking that God needs a little help from us. We might even get to the point where we start going against God's Word because we think our own way might be better and will help hurry things along. That's what Sarah did when she told her maid, Hagar, that Hagar should get pregnant. And then she, Sarah, would just take the baby. Sarah even tried to pass this scheme off as God's plan.

To make a long story short, Sarah's plan backfired. Hagar gave birth to Ishmael, and Sarah's people and Hagar's people—the Israelites and the Arabs—are still fighting to this day. And it all started with Sarah's deep bitterness and resentment toward Hagar—which happened *after* Hagar did what Sarah told her to do. What a mess!

Have you ever gotten impatient waiting for something to happen and then decided to speed things along by doing it your own way? What was the result? How would you do things differently next time?

_____

_____

_____

_____

_____

_____

_____

_____

_____

_____

At this point, you might be wondering how Sarah ended up a kingdom hero. Good question! But that's why Hebrews 11:11, which we'll read in a moment, is such an important verse. It reminds us that it's never too late to turn back to God. It's never too late to become a kingdom hero. No person has made too many mistakes, committed too many sins, or gone too far off course that they can't return to God and start living a life of faith.

Sarah doubted, so she tried to bring God's promises about in her own way. She took matters into her own hands. Maybe she was a little bit of a control freak. But she was able to learn from her mistakes. Hebrews 11:11 says, "And by faith even Sarah, who was past childbearing age, was enabled to bear children because she considered him faithful who had made the promise."

KINGDOM HERO SPOTLIGHT
Joseph

Joseph lived out a strong life of faith on behalf of his family and the people of Egypt. And he demonstrated his faith in many ways—including being willing to forgive his brothers for selling him into slavery. His forgiveness came in a heart rooted in the belief that God is good. As he said to his brothers in Genesis 50:20, "You intended to harm me, but God intended it for good to accomplish what is now being done, the saving of many lives."

Joseph also spared his family from starvation, along with all of the Egyptians, through his ability to live as a true disciple of God in a land of people who didn't follow Him. He interpreted Pharaoh's dreams, which allowed him to stockpile food to nourish the Israelites during a worldwide famine. And his wisdom and leadership skills helped him fit into another culture so much that he rose to a position of great national influence.

By the time Joseph reached the end of his life, he was known as a kingdom hero in the hearts and minds of his fellow Israelites.

ANYTHING IS POSSIBLE!

Sarah eventually discovered that, even though what God said didn't match her reality, she could still trust Him by faith. But she didn't learn that lesson right away. When God told Sarah she would have a son within a year, do you know what she did? She laughed! And this wasn't a laughing-with-excitement kind of laugh. This was an I-don't-believe-it kind of laugh. You know, kind of a sarcastic laugh. (Think "rolling eyes" emoji.)

> Abraham and Sarah were already very old, and Sarah was past the age of childbearing. So Sarah laughed to herself as she thought, "After I am worn out and [Abraham] is old, will I now have [a son]?"

> Then the LORD said to Abraham, "Why did Sarah laugh and say, 'Will I really have a child, now that I am old?' Is anything too hard for the LORD? I will return to you at the appointed time next year, and Sarah will have a son" (Genesis 18:11-14).

Why did Sarah laugh? Because she thought it was crazy that she could be 90 years old and still have a child. She didn't believe that God could do it. She had lost faith. In fact, she thought that God's promise had become ridiculous. I mean, if you think about it, can you imagine your 90-year-old great-grandma having a kid? It sounds impossible!

But anything's possible with God.

Like God said in Genesis 18:14,
"Is anything too hard for the LORD?"

God's promise for Sarah may have been impossible given the facts. But He wasn't focusing on the facts when He gave her the promise. Remember, nothing is too difficult for the God who created the earth out of nothing.

Still wondering how Sarah became a kingdom hero? I mean, she laughed at God's promises. She outright questioned them. And she tried to manipulate the situation and take over and make things happen her own way. But, thankfully, God didn't give up on Sarah. He was patient with her and gave her the opportunity to learn a few more things in order to strengthen her faith.

GROW YOUR FAITH

We know God didn't give up on Sarah because we see the lessons Sarah learned between the time she laughed and the time she gave birth to Isaac. God allowed Sarah to see enough of His hand moving in situations all around her so that her faith would grow. And so that she could believe the impossible.

God will do the same thing for you when He sees you waiting for Him to do the things He's promised you He will do. Sometimes He sends someone into your life who has a similar story, and you learn that He can do the impossible. Or suddenly you see another path you can take—one that God wants you to walk on. You might even read a new story in the Bible—or a story you've read before but you suddenly see that story in another way. You understand how it relates to your own life. And your faith begins to grow.

Write down some good ways to grow your faith. If Sarah and the other kingdom heroes could grow their faith, so can you!

_____

_____

_____

_____

_____

_____

_____

_____

_____

_____

Sarah's faith grew as she saw God at work in the lives of the people around her. In fact, her faith grew so much that she learned how to let go. She let go of trying to manipulate her situation. She let go of laughing at the impossible. She let go of not having faith. When she let go and let God take control, Sarah experienced her miracle. And she became a kingdom hero.

> Now the Lord was gracious to Sarah as he had said, and the Lord did for Sarah what he had promised. Sarah became pregnant and bore a son to Abraham in his old age, at the very time God had promised him. Abraham gave the name Isaac to the son Sarah bore him. When his son Isaac was eight days old, Abraham circumcised him, as God commanded him. Abraham was a hundred years old when his son Isaac was born to him.

Sarah said, "God has brought me laughter, and everyone who hears about this will laugh with me." And she added, "Who would have said to Abraham that Sarah would nurse children? Yet I have born him a son in his old age" (Genesis 21:1-7).

There's a saying that goes, "He who laughs last, laughs best." The last laugh is always the one that remains. Well, Sarah and God shared this last and best laugh together. In fact, the name Isaac literally means "laughter."

God put Sarah in a situation that seemed hopeless so she could stretch her faith. And He did it so He would get the glory. Sarah tried to make things happen on her own, but that never works out. God wanted Sarah to trust Him and to wait on Him. As a kingdom hero, Sarah learned to be patient and wait for God with hope and expectation. The first time we saw Sarah laughing, it wasn't nice laughter. It was making-fun-of-God laughter. But the second time she laughed, it was out of awe at God's ability to make the impossible happen. It was joyful laughter.

Sometimes God puts your back up against the wall—not to be mean but to let you see that He is truly God. When Sarah's back was up against the wall, it gave her the chance to grow and mature in her faith, even if she did make some mistakes along the way. In fact, Sarah had made a mess of things! But her story proves that it's never too late for God to show up and do the impossible. Even if you don't believe He can do it. *Especially* if you don't believe He can do it!

STICK WITH OTHER BELIEVERS

As a kingdom hero, Sarah had learned the skill of having faith, which ultimately produced her miracle. But she also learned that part of having faith was respecting and honoring the people around you. When she made the decision to listen to God and have faith in His plan, she stopped trying to manipulate others and started working with them.

It's super common to blame someone else when things don't go your way. You miss your band concert because you have the flu—so you blame your brother who gave you the flu. You don't win the election for class president—so you blame others for not voting for you, even though the kid who won ran a better campaign. You don't get to sleep over at your friend's house because you watched TV instead of doing your chores—so you blame your parents for being "unfair." You can't go back and change things, so you get mad and blame someone.

Who do you blame when things don't go your way? (Be honest!) Write down ways *you* can take responsibility for your mistakes and words you can say (like "my mistake," "my fault," "I was wrong") instead of blaming others. _____

_____

_____

_____

_____

_____

_____

_____

_____

_____

_____

_____

_____

Whatever the situation, blame has no place in a kingdom hero's heart. Part of having faith involves living according to the highest rule in the kingdom—the rule of love. First Corinthians 13:7 says love "always protects, always trusts, always hopes, always perseveres."

Love doesn't blame.

When Sarah stopped trying to solve the problem herself and stopped blaming others, she got her miracle.

Sarah got what she desired most. She got her son. What's more, the Bible tells us that Sarah didn't die until she was 127 years old. She had her son when she was 90 years old. That means she got to be with Isaac for 37 years. She got to experience the joy of the family she'd always hoped for.

God's Word says that if we follow the example of Sarah, honoring those we are to honor and trusting God, we get to live without fear. We get to let go of our worries about the future and about what might or might not happen. When you have faith that God will do what He says He's going to do, God will make His promises real in your life. And you'll have plenty of time to enjoy them!

GOD GIVES US TIME

Sarah's story teaches us that no matter how much time has gone by or how long we've been waiting, we can still hope in God. We should never give up. When it comes to God, we should always believe the impossible.

> *Nothing is too hard for God to pull off, whenever He chooses to do it.*

Faith is never just about your emotions—the way you feel. Faith is also about actions—the things you do. Sometimes that means doing something you're uncomfortable doing. Sometimes it means continuing to trust God, even if the facts don't make sense. Sometimes it means waiting for what can seem like *forever*.

Faith looks different in different situations. To live as a kingdom hero means you choose to stay so close to God that pleasing Him becomes the most important thing in your life. Honoring Him becomes the way you roll. Getting to know Him and learning more about His ways becomes your normal flow.

Be a kingdom hero like Sarah.

Live by faith.

Dream big.

Believe the impossible.

6

MOSES

Making the Right Choice

Moses has an awesome kingdom-hero story, and it starts right from the beginning of his life. You might remember how his mother hid him in the river, kept out of sight by a tall bunch of wild reeds. Hebrews 11:23 shows how Moses started out his life of adventure: "By faith Moses' parents hid him for three months after he was born, because they saw he was no ordinary child, and they were not afraid of the king's edict."

Not afraid. Those two words sum up how Moses grew up. His parents were "not afraid." They lived with faith over fear. They passed down a legacy of belief to their son.

But even more than that, Moses's parents' lack of fear—despite the fact that they lived at a time when people were very evil—saved Moses's life. They chose to hide their baby boy so he would not be killed, as the king of Egypt had ordered all Hebrew baby boys to be killed as soon as they were born.

Then, when Moses grew too big to hide, they came up with a plan to keep him safe and secure.

The strategy, as you might remember, involved placing Moses in a basket, in the Nile River near the place where Pharaoh's daughter bathed, accompanied by her maids. Moses's parents knew he was a beautiful baby, and they figured that Pharaoh's daughter would think so too. They were right. When she heard the crying infant, she "opened [the basket] and saw the baby. He was crying, and she felt sorry for him. 'This is one of the Hebrew babies,' she said" (Exodus 2:6).

Now, Moses's parents knew that Pharaoh's daughter wouldn't be able to raise a child on her own. In that culture, the servants raised the babies. So they placed Moses's big sister, Miriam, where she could keep an eye on the basket and then pop out and introduce herself when it was retrieved.

The plan went perfectly, and when Miriam offered to find someone to help nurse the baby and care for him in the palace, Pharaoh's daughter agreed. Miriam was more than willing to offer her own mother to do just that.

> Then his sister asked Pharaoh's daughter, "Shall I go and get one of the Hebrew women to nurse the baby for you?"
>
> "Yes, go," she answered. So the girl went and got the baby's mother. Pharaoh's daughter said to her, "Take this baby and nurse him for me, and I will pay you." So the woman took the baby and nursed him. When the child grew older, she took him to Pharaoh's daughter and he became her son. She named him Moses, saying, "I drew him out of the water" (Exodus 2:7-10).

Not only was Moses's life spared, but his own mother was also paid to nurse him. What a perfect solution! And what a perfect example of what it means to live by faith.

> *Living by faith means choosing to follow*
> *God's plan and then watching Him work*
> *it out for your good and others' benefit.*

MOSES DECIDES

The way Moses was raised made a big impact on him. Hebrews 11:24-25 says, "By faith Moses, when he had grown up, refused to be known as the son of Pharaoh's daughter. He chose to be mistreated along with the people of God rather than to enjoy the fleeting pleasures of sin."

What made Moses decide to follow God when he knew that God's way would be much harder? First, while his mother was nursing Moses, she used that time to teach him about what really mattered. Through her teachings, Moses developed a heart for his own people, the Israelites. He had faith that what his mother had taught him was true. In fact, when (according to Acts 7:23) Moses was around 40 years old, he refused to be called the son of Pharaoh's daughter any longer.

Moses paid a price for that decision. At that point, he had it all—money, power, education, friends, comfort. Life was good! Yet despite all that, he made a choice to no longer be associated with the Egyptians. He made this choice based on all the times his mother had reminded him of who he really was and where he had come from. He wasn't like the others. He was an Israelite, and God had something special planned for his life.

Because of the influence of his mother, Moses learned all about God's future plans for him. Moses had everything a person could ever want, but he knew that God expected more from him. And so he made a choice.

Moses made the choice to follow God's plan and lead the Israelites to the Promised Land. It would not be an easy journey, but Moses had faith that this was the right thing to do. And his choice led God's chosen people to freedom.

Who has taught you important lessons about God and life? Write their names down here and then remember to listen when those people talk!

CHOOSE YOUR KINGDOM

When my kids were young, our family liked to go to Disneyland. The kids loved to watch Mickey Mouse, Minnie Mouse, and especially Goofy on TV, and we thought it would be fun for them to meet those characters "in person." It was a long drive from Texas to California, but we finally made it to the Magic Kingdom.

We were there during the peak of vacation season, so the place was packed. After a while, my wife and I got so caught up in all of the fun and excitement that—I'll admit it—we let down our guard. We'd stopped paying close attention to where our kids were, and before we knew it, our youngest son, Jonathan, was no longer with us.

Jonathan had wandered off when we weren't watching. We looked all over but we couldn't find him. Panicked, I went to a security station to report that my son was missing. Soon the security staff was also looking for him.

In a place where there should have been nothing but fun and happiness, we found ourselves worried and scared. The Magic Kingdom hadn't turned out to be that magical after all. Eventually, we found Jonathan in a toy store looking at all the displays. We were grateful to have found him but exhausted by our search.

We had two problems that day in Disneyland. First, Jonathan had become distracted by the sights and sounds of the kingdom he was in. Second, *we'd* become distracted by the sights and sounds of the kingdom we were in. We'd all become distracted by the imagery, music, rides, and thrills in the Magic Kingdom. In fact, we'd become so focused on that kingdom that we lost our focus on what mattered most—our own little child.

If we don't focus on God's kingdom—which is what matters most—we can easily be pulled away by the lure of another kingdom. The kingdom of darkness wants nothing more than to pull us away from God's kingdom of light. It might disguise itself as excitement and fun, but it's not. The only real joy is found in God's kingdom of light.

Keep your focus on the *real* Magic Kingdom—God's kingdom.

STANDING WITH GOD

Once you make the clear choice to stand with God, you will run into problems. Some people will make fun of you. You might find yourself uncomfortable with certain people or situations. You will sometimes feel frustrated and alone. Following God isn't always easy! But it *is* always worth it.

If you think that life is a popularity contest, the choice to follow God as His kingdom hero is going to be a really hard choice for you. That's because kingdom heroes care about what God thinks, not about what other people think. The apostle Paul said it pretty intensely: "In fact, everyone who wants to live a godly life in Christ Jesus will be persecuted" (2 Timothy 3:12).

At some point, things will get a little rough if you choose to follow Jesus. You might not be in the "in-crowd" anymore. You might not get picked to be team captain. Some people might even try to bully you. (If this happens, please talk to an adult. It's *not* okay to put up with some things, and bullying is one of those things.)

But please don't worry. Following Jesus is the best thing you could ever do! And God promises He will be there for you—always.

This doesn't mean you will always be a perfect Christian or will always do the right thing. Sometimes, sin can be enjoyable or fun. Sometimes, doing the wrong thing with a group of people can seem to bond you. But it's not a bond that will last. It might feel good at the moment, but it's not the best way to build a friendship.

While sin can be fun in the moment, it's a passing pleasure at best. That's why sin can be addictive. A person has to keep sinning in order to experience sin's highest level of enjoyment. Take gossip. It might be fun at first to be known as the person who has all the dirt and who spreads all the rumors. It gets your attention, right? But then other people start to expect that from you. And you realize that the people who are super into drama aren't the nicest people to hang out with. Eventually, your gossip gets back to others, and suddenly everyone is upset with you. You have no idea how to get out of this mess! The sin of gossip might have been fun and gotten you lots of attention at the start, but it made things so much worse in the end.

Moses made the decision *not* to get caught up in the temporary fun of sin. He looked at the pros and cons. And he realized that if he sided with

God and His people, he would be setting himself up for the greater reward up ahead. That was a reward Moses did not want to miss out on!

THE REWARD

Rewards are fun, aren't they? You can set a goal—like reading a certain number of books over the summer or keeping your room clean for a whole month—and if you reach your goal, there's a reward waiting for you at the end. Maybe a pizza party or an ice cream sundae or a special shopping trip.

Make a list of goals and rewards. Write down three to five goals. Now, think of a reward you will get when you meet your goal—a dinner out, a new shirt, a family bike ride. Write down the reward too. (Be sure to talk to your parents if the reward will cost money or if it involves other family members.)_____

_____

_____

_____

_____

_____

_____

_____

_____

_____

Moses knew that a reward from God would be far better than any reward he could receive here on earth. He understood what truly mattered, which is why he made the choice he did. He picked a side. He picked God's side.

But I don't think Moses was thinking only of an eternal reward. He had been listening to his mother's voice ever since he was born. She'd given him the history of the Hebrew people. She'd told him the stories of Abraham and the agreement that he and God had made—that one day they would have an entire nation. She'd shared with him the promise of a land all their own and told him that someone would need to lead the Israelites there. We don't know for sure, but she probably told Moses that he was the one to do it. After all, that's why he had been placed in the Egyptian palace and given a position of power.

Moses was a leader. He was smart. He'd been spared and chosen by God Himself. Moses's mother didn't want her son to fall so in love with the world that he would miss out on God's plan for his life. So she talked to him. A lot.

The rewards of God are greater than the treasures of man. But unless you really and truly believe that, you won't make wise decisions like Moses did. You'll wind up hanging out with the world instead of giving yourself fully to God.

God's rewards are greater than any of earth's treasures!

Because of his faith, Moses made up his mind to go for God's reward. Hebrews 11:27 says, "By faith he left Egypt, not fearing the king's anger; he persevered because he saw him who is invisible." Moses chose God over an earthly king.

KINGDOM HERO SPOTLIGHT
Deborah (Judges 4–5)

Deborah was one of the most influential kingdom heroes of the Old Testament era. Her job was to be a judge, and her office was one of the coolest work environments you can imagine. While she sat under a palm tree, people came to her with their arguments and disputes. The wise Deborah met people at the palm tree, listened to what they said, and then made decisions about what to do—she "judged" the situation. (Between clients, she could probably even nap beneath the palm tree!)

During Deborah's time, her people—the Israelites—had been oppressed for many years. Things eventually reached a point where Deborah, who was super in touch with God, decided that something needed to be done. She sent a message to a man named Barak and told him to gather 10,000 troops to go fight the enemy. Barak responded the way a lot of us respond when someone tells us to do something—he didn't want to go. But Deborah insisted to Barak that God wanted them to do this and that He would be with them.

After the Israelites won, there was peace in the land for 40 years. Besides ushering in an era of peace, Deborah also was special in another way. She was the only Old Testament judge who was also a prophet. Smart, fair, and faithful, Deborah was a kingdom hero all-star!

THE CALLING

Have you ever just had a feeling that you should do something? Like you should talk to a certain friend. Or do a certain thing. Or pray about a certain person or situation. When we're tuned in to God, He helps us become aware of certain important things.

This is what happened with Moses. Acts 7:25-30 says:

> Moses thought that his own people would realize that God was using him to rescue them, but they did not. The next day Moses came upon two Israelites who were fighting. He tried to reconcile them by saying, "Men, you are brothers; why do you want to hurt each other?"

> But the man who was mistreating the other pushed Moses aside and said, "Who made you ruler and judge over us? Are you thinking of killing me as you killed the Egyptian yesterday?" When Moses heard this, he fled to Midian, where he settled as a foreigner and had two sons.

> After forty years had passed, an angel appeared to Moses in the flames of a burning bush in the desert near Mount Sinai.

You've probably heard this story about the burning bush. And you might know how the story ends. Moses learned to trust God. By trusting God, he was able to access God's power, which helped him lead the Hebrew people to freedom.

Like Moses, you might feel shaky in your faith right now. You might be unsure of what to do. You might be feeling super confused about school and friends and your future and… everything! No matter what, God has confidence in you. And if you have confidence in Him—and trust Him—He can raise you up and strengthen you to complete great works for Him.

Like Moses, you can dream big as to what God can and will do through you for others. There really is no limit to what you can do as a kingdom hero if you commit yourself to God's kingdom plan and seek to serve Him.

Make the right choice—the choice to follow God's plan for your life—and discover how it makes life better for yourself and everyone around you.

7

RAHAB

Taking a Risk

M ost of our kingdom heroes have been Israelites, but Rahab wasn't. She was a Gentile—a non-Jewish person. In fact, her people were the enemies of the Israelites. On top of that, her family didn't worship God. She came from a family with a history of pagan worship. The first two letters of her name were even chosen in honor of the Canaanite god, Ra. She'd been marked for his service at birth, branded for idolatry. From the start, her parents had wanted her to be connected to this pagan god.

Not only did Rahab grow up in a pagan family but she also grew up in a pagan culture that knew no boundaries on going against God's Word. Rahab's culture wasn't just a little bit different from the Israelites. It was entirely different!

GO ALL-IN

Have you ever taken a risk? Auditioning for the school play is taking a risk. Trying out for the elite club soccer team is a risk. Even introducing yourself to a potential new friend is a risk. In all of these things, you don't know 100 percent what the result will be. You might not get a role in the play (or at least not the role you want). You might not make the team. The new person might not become your friend.

But if you don't go all-in and take the risk, you know for sure what will happen. You won't be in the play—at all. You won't be playing soccer—at all. The new person won't be your friend—at all. So why not try? Sometimes the biggest risks result in the greatest rewards. You just never know where something can take you!

Kingdom heroes know what it's like to take risks. The heroes we read about in the Bible knew what it was like to put all of their eggs in God's basket. They went all-in, and because they did, they were rewarded by God.

A SPY STORY

Despite not following God, Rahab played an instrumental role in God's divine plan for the world. And her story is pretty legendary.

> Then Joshua son of Nun secretly sent two spies from Shittim. "Go, look over the land," he said, "especially Jericho." So they went and entered the house of a prostitute named Rahab and stayed there.
>
> The king of Jericho was told, "Look, some of the Israelites have come here tonight to spy out the land." So the king of Jericho sent this message to Rahab: "Bring out the men who came to you and entered your house, because they have come to spy out the whole land."
>
> But the woman had taken the two men and hidden them. She said, "Yes, the men came to me, but I did not know where they had come from. At dusk, when it was time to close the city gate, they left. I don't know which way they went. Go after them quickly. You may catch up with them." (But she had taken them up to the roof and hidden them under the stalks of flax she had laid out on the roof.) So the men set out in pursuit of the spies on the road that leads to the fords of the Jordan, and as soon as the pursuers had gone out, the gate was shut (Joshua 2:1-7).

Rahab's home was easy to get to, which is why the Israelites were able to send two spies to her. The men snuck into Rahab's home, and then someone spied on them and reported them to the king. Which caused the king to send word to Rahab to turn over the enemies' spies. Rahab responded by pretending that she didn't know what the king was talking about. She said that the spies had already left, even though she still had them there hidden on the roof.

Yep, Rahab lied.

How could Rahab be a kingdom hero if she lied? After all, isn't lying bad?

Let's see what the Bible says about a choice we must sometimes make.

MAKE THE CHOICE THAT GIVES GOD THE GLORY

We all know that lying is a sin. In fact, the Bible clearly tells us that lying is a sin. So why did Rahab lie? And how did this choice make her a kingdom hero?

Rahab knew that turning these two men in as spies would get them killed. She was faced with two difficult choices (both of which would involve sinning): *Lie*, saving the men's lives. Or *tell the truth*, turning them in to be killed. She decided to lie. Here's why she made that decision.

If two sins are the only options you have, you should choose the one that will bring God the greatest glory. You have to make the choice that will honor Him the most. Rahab chose to hide the spies and lie to the king's messengers to get them off the trail of the men she was hiding. She chose to save their lives.

Always make the choice that will bring God the greatest glory.

Another way to say it: Always side with the good guys. Always side with God's people.

Here's a little more about Rahab and the spies:

> Before the spies lay down for the night, [Rahab] went up on the roof and said to them, "I know that the LORD has given you this land and that a great fear of you has fallen on us, so that all who live in this country are melting in fear because of you. We have heard how the LORD dried up the water of the Red Sea for you when you came out of Egypt, and what you did to Sihon and Og, the two kings of the Amorites east of the Jordan, whom you completely destroyed. When we heard of it, our hearts melted in fear and everyone's courage failed because of you, for the LORD your God is God in heaven above and on the earth below" (Joshua 2:8-11).

Essentially, Rahab let the men know that she knew their God was the real deal. His reputation had reached their city walls. Her people had been told about the miraculous journey out of Egypt. They'd heard of the parting of the Red Sea. The Israelites had become known as a people whose God worked wonders on their behalf.

Based on what she did and where she lived, Rahab was in a position to hear a lot of things. And the information she heard needed to be taken seriously. Her sources were reliable. So, as a result of what she'd heard and who she believed, Rahab made the risky choice to flip. She decided to switch sides. In faith, she aligned herself with the one true God.

Rahab stood alone in this choice. She and her friends had all heard the same things about the Hebrews' God, but only Rahab chose to make a move based on what they'd heard. She was the only one who made the risky and radical decision to get out of danger while she could. She was the only one who chose to follow God's plan.

> Have you ever been in a situation where you had to make a really difficult choice? Write down what you remember about that situation. What did you choose? What helped you make that choice? Would you make the same choice now?_____
>
> _____
>
> _____
>
> _____
>
> _____
>
> _____
>
> _____
>
> _____
>
> _____
>
> _____
>
> _____
>
> _____

Rahab's story reminds us that sometimes siding with God means siding against our friends or against the world where we live. Every kingdom hero reaches a point where they have to choose Christ or choose the crowd. You have to choose God or the group. You must choose between the King and the culture. This might show up at school, in your friendships, in your neighborhood, or at your activities.

Your choice will reveal your faith.

When you stand with God, not everyone is going to like it. You may feel all alone when you make a faith decision, but those faith decisions are super important. For Rahab, her faith decision was a matter of life or death. Had Rahab sided with the culture, she would have gone down with the walls. She and her family would have lost their lives the day those trumpets blew. But because she chose to place her faith in God, she saved both herself and her family.

We can read Rahab's words and see a little of her thought process in Joshua 2:12-14:

> "Now then, please swear to me by the Lord that you will show kindness to my family, because I have shown kindness to you. Give me a sure sign that you will spare the lives of my father and mother, my brothers and sisters, and all who belong to them— and that you will save us from death."

> "Our lives for your lives!" the men assured her. "If you don't tell what we are doing, we will treat you kindly and faithfully when the Lord gives us the land."

Rahab was smart. She knew what was about to happen in her land, and she believed the reputation of the God she'd heard about. And even though her neighbors felt secure behind fortified walls, she didn't. She'd heard the stories of the God who could divide an entire sea with His wind. So she told the two Israelite spies what she would do for them and then told them exactly what she wanted in return.

Write down Rahab's adventurous story in your own words. You can even draw pictures of what happened or write down the dialogue between Rahab and the spies like you would write a movie script. _____

_____

_____

_____

_____

_____

_____

_____

_____

_____

_____

_____

_____

_____

_____

_____

_____

KINGDOM HERO SPOTLIGHT

Joshua

Jericho was a walled city, fortified to such a degree that it was nearly impenetrable. The walls were so high and so wide that people could conduct chariot races on top of them. The city was locked up tight like a drum. Yet here came the Israelites to invade it, according to God's plan. And God's plan was nothing anyone had ever envisioned.

You may have already heard Joshua's story, but let's take another look at it.

Now the gates of Jericho were securely barred because of the Israelites. No one went out and no one came in.

Then the LORD said to Joshua, "See, I have delivered Jericho into your hands, along with its king and its fighting men. March around the city once with all the armed men. Do this for six days. Have seven priests carry trumpets of rams' horns in front of the ark. On the seventh day, march around the city seven times, with the priests blowing the trumpets. When you hear them sound a long blast on the trumpets, have the whole army give a loud shout; then the wall of the city will collapse and the army will go up, everyone straight in" (Joshua 6:1-5).

In this battle plan, God gave Joshua a strategy no military leader had ever thought of before—or since, probably because any troop would look like fools carrying it out. He told Joshua and his men to march around the wall for seven days, and on the seventh day, they were to go around it seven times. And they were also supposed to blow their trumpets and scream a shout of praise!

Now, if Joshua had been looking at normal instructions in the military manual, he never would have taken this kind of risk. It just wouldn't make any sense. But remember, when God puts you in a position that doesn't make sense, that's because He wants you to see that He is God and that He can do anything!

Joshua didn't complain. He and the rest of the Israelites put on their marching boots and started walking. Finally, after a week, they blew their trumpets and screamed. And as we all know, the walls came tumbling down!

Joshua's story shows us that God can knock down something you can't knock down on your own or turn something around you can't turn around yourself—even if it means doing some-thing strange. That's because God sees the end from the begin-ning. And He can pull off things we wouldn't even know to ask Him to do because the idea never crossed our minds.

It's not hard to be a kingdom hero when you realize who's on your side. When God has your back, it doesn't matter that it's against a wall. Just say the word (or blow the trumpet), and that wall will fall faster than a deck of cards stacked high.

HERE'S THE DEAL

A lot of people want to make a deal with God on the condition that He does His part first. But that's not faith. Rahab was willing to put herself and her family at risk because of her faith that God would be loyal in holding up His end of the bargain later. She put her faith first—with actions.

If you want God to do something, you need to act first. You need to let Him know what you're willing to do for Him in faith. Because without faith it's impossible to please Him. He's not going to show you what to do until you walk forward. You need to show that you trust Him.

God doesn't mind answering our prayers—in fact, He loves to do this! He wants to respond to our requests. He wants to do things for us. He wants to give us what we ask for. But we need to act too. Even if other people think we're weird.

As the Israelites marched around the wall of Jericho for the first six days, I'm sure a lot of people were making fun of them. Yet Rahab didn't care. She stayed true to her beliefs and never caved to a culture of mean words and insults. She stood strong. She stood tall. And when the wall eventually did fall, she was one of the last few standing.

Here's something crazy. Rahab's home was *in* the wall. The walls of Jericho collapsed, but one part of the wall remained intact—the part that housed Rahab. She trusted God in advance of the crisis, so that when the crisis happened, she and her family were safe.

Is there something you've been putting off doing because it seems too scary? It could be anything from talking to a new person to trying a new food to deciding to switch to a different school. Write down three positive but "risky" things that pop into your mind. Then write down some actions you can take to make these things happen!

_____

_____

_____

_____

_____

_____

_____

_____

_____

_____

_____

_____

MOVE THOSE FEET

Rahab shows up in the New Testament as an example of what faith truly looks like:

> You see that a person is considered righteous by what they do and not by faith alone.

In the same way, was not even Rahab the prostitute considered
righteous for what she did when she gave lodging to the spies
and sent them off in a different direction? As the body without
the spirit is dead, so faith without deeds is dead (James 2:24-26).

Rahab's decision to hide the spies and send them out of the city another
way so they wouldn't get caught not only saved the spies but led to God saving Rahab and her family as well. When we decide, as Rahab did, that we're
going to make choices based on our faith in God—even if that means going
against our culture and the crowd—we'll see God doing amazing things in
our lives. If He did it for Rahab, He can do it for us. Her story is a story for
everyone!

It doesn't matter how many mistakes you've made. (Trust me, Rahab
made *a lot* of mistakes in her life!) You are made in the image of the King
Himself. No matter how many bad things you've done, if you choose God by
faith—over the crowd, circumstances, popularity, fear, money, and more—
He will care for you with His kindness and love. He will erase your past mistakes and show you a bright future. He will make you a kingdom hero.

Take the risk Rahab took.

Take the risk to do the right thing.

Take the risk to follow God's plan.

YOU!

8

YOU!

Becoming a Kingdom Hero

Hebrews 11:6 says, "Without faith it is impossible to please God, because anyone who comes to him must believe that he exists and that he rewards those who earnestly seek him." This verse makes it crystal clear that without faith, we won't see God. If we don't have faith, we can still know that God exists, but we won't necessarily experience His presence in our day-to-day lives. And we won't have a chance to become kingdom heroes. That's why God tells us in the Bible to live our lives by faith. He wants us to experience His love and His power. He wants to be a part of our lives. He wants to help us through everything we go through. But first we need to have faith.

Faith shows up in your actions. It shows up in your walk, not just your talk. Faith is made real when you choose to obey God, even when you don't understand what's going on or how it's all going to work out.

Faith shows up in your walk,
not just your talk.

Most people decide what they're going to do by what they see first. They want to know how a situation is going to turn out before they take any action. Yet faith doesn't work that way. Faith only works if you believe first.

Let me give you an example of how faith—or actually a *lack* of faith—works in the animal kingdom. The African impala is a magnificent animal. I got to see one on a trip I took to South Africa several years ago. The African impala can jump ten feet straight up in the air. It can also jump outwardly up to 30 feet.

Yet if you put an African impala with all of its beauty, power, and ability behind a three-foot-high wall, expecting it to leap over it high and long, it will remain imprisoned there for life. This is due to one flaw: It won't jump if it can't see where it will land. It limits its own movements to what it can see. While the ability is there to become free, an African impala won't act on that ability because it won't trust what it cannot see. It doesn't have enough faith.

SALVATION AND FAITH

Sometimes we mix up salvation and faith. Let me explain.

When you accept Jesus Christ as your personal Savior by placing your faith in Him alone for the forgiveness of your sins, you are given eternal life. But while you trust Christ *through* faith, you are now supposed to live your life *by* faith. These are two very different things. Trusting Christ for salvation is like receiving a gift. Living by faith is *doing* something. Living by faith is *acting* on what you believe.

Accepting Christ as your Savior takes you to heaven. Living by faith brings heaven's power here to you on earth. It allows you to see God show up in your life.

> *You get to heaven by accepting Christ*
> *as your Savior. You get heaven's power*
> *here on earth when you live by faith.*

Unfortunately, people often confuse salvation and faith. As a result, many Christians don't live by faith. Instead, they live by sight while calling it faith. They say they trust God to do it. They wait on God for every move. They don't do anything for themselves. They expect God to do everything for them. Yet while God did everything for you and me through the gift of salvation, He does expect us to do the work of faith. He does expect us to act on our faith.

Living by faith means doing things *before* you see results. Living by faith means taking the leap and deciding to do what God has called you to do—even if you can't see ahead of time how it's going to turn out. That's how God works in your life, and that's how you get to experience His power.

In your own words, explain how *salvation* and *faith* are two different things. _____

_____

_____

_____

_____

_____

_____

_____

_____

_____

_____

IT'S OKAY TO BE DIFFERENT!

Living by faith sometimes makes you seem different. You may even appear weird to others—like Noah did. But those who live by faith are people of whom the world is not worthy (Hebrews 11:38). What does that mean—that the world is "not worthy" of certain people? It's when they live so connected to God that those who physically live with them on earth rarely understand what they're doing. Regular people think they're odd. They think they've lost their minds. They call them fanatics. Freaks. Or any other not-so-nice name people can come up with.

The world is not worthy of people who truly live by faith. It's not worthy of people who live their lives according to how God wants them to live. Those who live with an eternal perspective outwit, outplay, and outlast those who don't. Hebrews 11:39-40 says:

> These were all commended for their faith, yet none of them received what had been promised, since God had planned something better for us so that only together with us would they be made perfect.

None of those just mentioned—the kingdom heroes who had gained approval through their faith—received what was promised in this life. Many of the Old Testament kingdom heroes did not get what they were looking for. For example, Abraham never got to own the land God had promised him. He got to wander on it, but he never owned it. He got to see God work, but in his lifetime he didn't get to see everything God had promised him. But God still kept His promise.

When you choose to obey God even though you can't see what will happen ahead of time, God will work everything out according to His perfect plan. But you need to step out in faith. God's rewards don't come to you simply because you want them. They come to you because you live your life by His truth and His Word. They come to you because you put pleasing God above pleasing people—and even pleasing yourself. They come to you because you're not afraid to be different.

Describe a time when you felt different from everyone else around you. What was it that made you feel different? How did things turn out? Remember, sometimes it's okay to be different—especially when you're being different for God! _____

_____

_____

_____

_____

_____

_____

_____

_____

_____

_____

_____

_____

_____

As you've probably noticed by now, the kingdom heroes in the Bible were people who faced some pretty scary situations! Many—if not all—of them felt like giving up at one point. But they stuck with God. They stayed connected to Him. They followed His lead—even when they didn't really want to. Even when nobody else did.

The stories of the kingdom heroes inspire us. And they help us in our own journey as kingdom heroes. Hebrews 12:1-3 tells us more about being a kingdom hero:

> Therefore, since we are surrounded by such a great cloud of witnesses, let us throw off everything that hinders and the sin that so easily entangles. And let us run with perseverance the race marked out for us, fixing our eyes on Jesus, the pioneer and perfecter of faith. For the joy set before him he endured the cross, scorning its shame, and sat down at the right hand of the throne of God. Consider him who endured such opposition from sinners, so that you will not grow weary and lose heart.

God tells us that we are not supposed to lose heart. What does that mean? Losing heart is like a runner becoming exhausted to the point of collapse.

The runner loses all strength, energy, and even motivation to continue. To lose heart is to say, "Even though I want to go on, I just can't go any farther."

But the Bible gives us example after example of kingdom heroes who were different. These heroes stood up against the dangers and difficulties of their time and kept going despite all the problems they were facing. These kingdom heroes didn't lose heart.

They did it. They became kingdom heroes. They didn't throw in the towel. They risked. They set out. They believed. They stood up. They made choices based on what they truly believed in. And they lived out their faith.

WHAT DO YOU BELIEVE IN?

Faith is only as powerful as the object or being we believe in. And the most powerful object or being to put your faith in is God and His Word. God is real. He's the object of our hope. And if we put our faith in Him, He will give us a lot!

Sometimes you'll hear athletes or other famous people make statements like "I believe," with a period at the end of that sentence. Well, believe in what? That's not a complete understanding of faith, because faith must include something real. It must include the thing you're grabbing hold of. Belief in believing is never enough. *What* do you believe in? There needs to be an answer.

Faith isn't just a feeling. It's not an attitude or a logo on your T-shirt or hat. It's more than a saying you post on social media. Faith is doing something because of what you believe. If your feet are still and you are not moving, you don't have faith. Only actions reveal true faith.

There's a major difference between a high jumper and a pole vaulter. The high jumper depends on her ability to jump over the bar. The pole vaulter, however, depends on the pole to propel her much higher than she could ever jump on her own. Faith is grabbing hold of Jesus as the pole you lean on, which will let you go higher so you can rise above everything. What are some things in your life that you can trust Jesus to help you "rise above"?

_____

_____

_____

_____

_____

_____

_____

_____

_____

_____

The kingdom heroes we are reading about remind us that if all hope is gone, we can still go on. That's because we know the One greater than ourselves. The kingdom heroes remind us that faith involves following God even when times are difficult.

It's easy to follow God when nothing is going wrong. It becomes a greater challenge when *everything* seems to go wrong. Yet God calls us to follow Him through the good times *and* the bad times. Then God will tell us, "Job well done!" Or as the Bible says, "Well done, good and faithful servant!" (Matthew 25:23).

Some people have chosen the world's ways over God's ways because they wanted something bigger. For example, some people choose to give up on following God because they're surrounding themselves with the wrong kind of friends. They're hanging out with people who don't follow Jesus and don't care about what the Bible says.

Why would you choose to hang out with someone who's headed in the wrong direction spiritually? Sure, you can be their friend. Even better, you can tell them all about Jesus! But make sure that your best friends—the people you spend the most time with—are friends who will help you grow closer to God.

Also important: Choose to surround yourself with friends and mentors who are older than you and have more life experience! Listen to the people who have been there and still came out with a win. Follow the people who have faith in God.

Make a list of friends and other people you know—family members, teachers, family friends, even social media influencers—who are following Jesus. Be sure to spend lots of time hanging out with and listening to these people!_____

_____

_____

_____

_____

_____

_____

_____

_____

_____

WORK TOGETHER

What you do on your own matters. But what you do as part of a group matters too. You can score 50 points in a basketball game, but if you don't play well with your team, you can still lose the game. You can do an awesome job on your part of the science fair project, but if the rest of the kids in your group do nothing, your project isn't going to be very successful.

One person's actions affect the people around them. But the actions of an entire group of people can make an even bigger difference—for good or for bad.

In the Old Testament, the Israelites needed to work together as a group if they wanted to reach the Promised Land. Hebrews 11:29-30 says:

> By faith the people passed through the Red Sea as on dry land; but when the Egyptians tried to do so, they were drowned.

By faith the walls of Jericho fell, after the army had marched around them for seven days.

Moses was the leader of the Israelites, but *all* of their actions mattered. They needed to work together—and to have faith—as a group in order for God's plan to work.

Think about when you've been in a situation where you needed to work with a group of people. What was hard about it? What did you like about it?

To work together successfully, you need to have a plan. And following God's plan is the best way to work together!

What are some things you like to do your own way? Does doing things your own way always work? How do you think God might want you to do things another way?

JOIN THE FAMILY

God wants every Christian to be part of a spiritual family. You don't need to go to church to hear a sermon. You can listen to a sermon on YouTube. You don't need to go to church to worship. You can worship by yourself or just listen to your favorite worship songs.

What church *does* give us is the opportunity to get to know a community of believers. Church gives us a group of other people who love God to hang out with, learn from, and grow with. God doesn't want you to go on the journey of faith alone. Hebrews 10:23-25 says:

> Let us hold unswervingly to the hope we profess, for he who promised is faithful. And let us consider how we may spur one another on toward love and good deeds, not giving up meeting together, as some are in the habit of doing, but encouraging one another—and all the more as you see the Day approaching.

These verses say that all of us who are believers need to be involved in each other's lives. We need to hang out with each other and inspire each other. That way, when someone is having a hard time, someone else will be there to help and encourage them.

Sometimes we have a hard time as kingdom heroes *because* of other people. If we hang out with the wrong kind of people, we slow down our own progress.

The question isn't always whether a certain person is "bad" or "good." The question is if they are holding you back from growing with God. Besides people, things—like TV or social media or anything you like to do—can hold you back from growing with God. Going to church gives you a ready-made community of people who are growing with God. Going to church gives you a family of believers.

A REALLY BIG SIN

The sin of *unbelief* is a really big sin. In fact, if you get rid of the sin of unbelief, you get rid of a lot of your other sins as a result. The sin of unbelief can make things really messy. It ties you up and keeps you bound in knots of fear, doubt, worry, control, grief, and resentment. We also know it as the sin of *faithlessness*—basically, not having faith. This one really big sin affects everything else in your life.

There's a story of a college student who wanted to do his laundry without spending a lot of time on it, so he laid out a bedsheet and dumped his dirty clothes on it. Then he took the four corners of the sheet and tied them together, making a bundle, and tossed the bundle into the washer. But while he thought he was making his clothes clean, he was actually trapping the dirt and spreading it around. His clothes came out of the washing machine even dirtier than they had gone into it because they'd been tangled together in one thing—the sheet.

The sin of faithlessness will show up in every part of your life. It will show up in your feelings. It will show up in your words. It will show up in your actions. It will show up in your health. It will show up in anything you do. Faithlessness spreads the filth of unbelief to every part of your life. It makes your whole life dirty and yucky.

That's why you need to have faith in God. That's why you need to be *faithful*. When you learn to believe God fully and do what He asks you to do, you will start to live as a kingdom hero! You'll be able to "run with perseverance the race marked out for [you]," as Hebrews 12:1 encourages. You'll be able to keep pace with this long-distance run called the Christian life. In Hebrews 12:2, you're told that you'll be able to do that by "fixing [y]our eyes on Jesus, the pioneer and perfecter of faith."

If you focus on the hard stuff you're going through, you won't be able to get through it very well. You have to focus beyond what's happening. You have to follow Jesus's example of looking past the pain. You need to focus on the goal. You need to focus on Jesus. You need to have faith.

I believe the sun exists. I imagine you believe that too. But I don't believe the sun exists because I am looking at it. (By the way, *never* look directly at the sun!) I believe it exists because I can see everything else due to its light. You and I may not physically see Jesus now, but when we focus on who He is and what He has done, we can make it through anything! What are some of your favorite stories about Jesus? How might they help you make it through tough times?

_____

_____

_____

_____

_____

_____

_____

_____

_____

_____

_____

_____

_____

_____

_____

_____

_____

_____

KINGDOM HERO SPOTLIGHT
You!

You get to write this kingdom hero spotlight because it's all about you! Tell the story of your walk with God. When did you first meet Him? When did you realize He needed to be the most important part of your life? What are some of the major events and big adventures you've had so far? How has God helped you during these times? Have fun writing your own kingdom hero story!

THE START AND THE FINISH

Jesus is described as both the pioneer and perfecter of our faith. What does this mean? To be the pioneer means He's the originator—the One who starts it all. To be the perfecter means He's the completer—the One who finishes it all. Starter and finisher. Jesus is both. He also gives us all we need for the in-between times too.

The Bible says Jesus was able to endure everything He went through because of "the joy set before Him" (Hebrews 12:2). What He saw and knew about the future motivated Him to keep going when His life got super hard.

Think about how school can sometimes get hard. Maybe it's the work itself that's hard. Or maybe you just find school kind of boring. Or maybe you don't get along with your teacher. No matter what the reason is, the idea of finishing and moving on to the next grade is what motivates you to push through all the studying and taking tests. Some classes are fun and some aren't so fun, but if you choose to focus on the end goal—getting good grades or moving on to summer vacation—you will be able to push through. If you see something good in the future, that will help motivate you to get the hard stuff done today.

God has a plan for you. It's a good plan! Your future is full of both good and hope. Jesus will give you the ability to keep going when times get tough. Not only that, but He'll also give you the ability to do more than you ever thought was possible. He's with you at the start, He's there at the finish, and He's right by your side for all the in-between moments.

NEVER GIVE UP

A little girl had been given a puzzle by her father. As she began to work on it, she started to cry because she couldn't get the pieces to fit together. She felt frustrated and wanted to quit.

Her father noticed her tears and asked her what was wrong. She said that she couldn't do the puzzle. It had too many pieces. It was too hard. Her father took the top off the box and turned it over so she could see the picture. The puzzle he had given her was a picture of Jesus. He said, "You've been trying to put the pieces together one by one. But I want you to keep looking at the picture on the box. Keep looking at the picture of Jesus. Instead of trying to figure out each individual piece, focus on the picture. It will help you make sense of the whole puzzle."

Life comes with a lot of pieces, and sometimes trying to figure them all out and put them all together seems way too hard. It's so much work that it can leave you crying. But you can make it a lot easier if you keep looking at Jesus. When we focus on loving Him, living for Him, and serving Him, all the rest of the confusing pieces of life fall into place. That's what it means to live by faith.

We've spent a lot of time learning about the kingdom heroes in the Bible, and now it's *your* turn. It's your turn to take what you've learned and start living your life as a modern-day kingdom hero. The kingdom heroes in the Bible have taught you all you need to know and have given you the keys to trusting in God and never giving up.

Give God your best.

Walk with God.

Activate your faith.

Pass the test.

Believe the impossible.

Make the right choice.

Take a risk.

Become a kingdom hero!

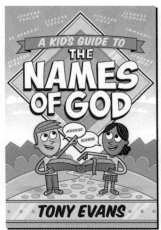
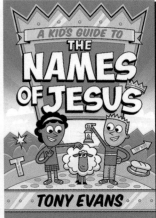
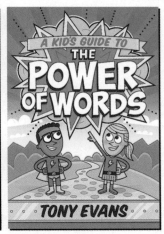

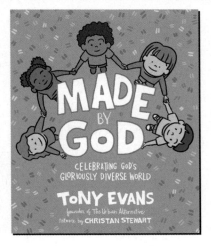